July 16, 1977

CARUSO

CARUSO

HIS LIFE IN PICTURES

FRANCIS ROBINSON

WITH

CARUSO DISCOGRAPHY

BY

JOHN SECRIST

BRAMHALL HOUSE : NEW YORK

0-517-036800
Copyright © MCMLVII by Francis Robinson
Library Of Congress Catalog Card Number: 57-9252
This edition is published by Bramhall House
a division of Clarkson N. Potter, Inc.
by arrangement with The Viking Press

a   b   c   d   e   f   g   h

Manufactured in the United States of America

To Mae

ACKNOWLEDGMENTS

THE AUTHOR'S PROFOUND THANKS GO TO ALL THOSE WHOSE NAMES APPEAR AS CREDIT lines in these pages, agencies as well as individuals. Because of them, the author had access to every picture of Caruso he had ever seen and might have wanted for use here except two.

Without the help of Mrs. Gloria Caruso and her sister, Mrs. William H. Porter, and Mr. and Mrs. Bruno Zirato this book would not have been possible. Marziale Sisca and his family and George Siegel were also infinitely helpful and encouraging.

Grateful acknowledgment is further made to the following: Irving Kolodin for his gifts of much valuable material, Martino Ceccanti, Margaret Anderson, Nora Shea, John Chapman, Betty Knop McGannon, Howard Taubman, Lucy R. Hurry, Hugh Wilson, Earle R. Lewis, Aimé Gerber, and the late Ray Vir Den.

Always ready with assistance at RCA Victor were Alan Kayes, George R. Marek, B. L. Aldridge, James Halpin, and Robert M. Jones. The librarians to whom the author is most beholden are: Edward N. Waters of the Library of Congress, John Austin Parker and F. W. Lane of Peabody Institute Library, Baltimore, and Philip L. Miller of The New York Public Library.

For certain unique photographs special thanks are due: Wayne T. Cottingham of the Associated Press, Mrs. John DeWitt Peltz, former editor of *Opera News,* May Davenport Seymour of the Museum of the City of New York, William H. Elsner of the California Palace of the Legion of Honor, Raymond Ericson of *Musical America,* Dr. Gid W. Waldrop of *Musical Courier,* Jack Thompson of the *Sunday Mirror,* D. Jay Culver, Daniel Blum, and particularly Alexander Eddy.

Special aid was generously forthcoming from the following: Dr. Franco Colombo, secretary of G. Ricordi & Co., Gaetano Cacciapuoti and Pasquale J. Simonelli of Naples, Roberto Bauer and Nicola Valente of Milan, Giorgio D'Andria and Dorcas Campbell on Caruso's Italian career; Ettore Bastianini, Georges Eid, Albert Wolf, Charles A. Jahant, Mitry's Photo-Optique of Cairo, and John W. Donald of King Features Syndicate on his appearances in Egypt; Edward Ivanian of the Ministry of Culture, U.S.S.R., Moscow, and Yuri I. Gouk, former cultural attaché at the Soviet Embassy in Washington, copies of the Russian photographs and programs; Prof. Eduardo Arnosi, Pedro Alfredo Diaz, and Department of Municipal Libraries of Buenos Aires; Hilary Watson on London; Rupert Allan on Monte Carlo; Anatole Heller on Paris; Leo Perper on

Lisbon; Max Rudolf on Prague; F. Masó Najó of the Gran Teatro Liceo, Barcelona, and István Molnár, cultural attaché of the Legation of the Hungarian People's Republic, Washington.

Dr. Fritz Stiedry of the Metropolitan Opera opened the way to help from the following sources in Germany: Dr. Walter Paproth of the Städtische Oper, Berlin; Dr. Martin G. Sarneck of the Kulturhistorisches Archiv, Berlin-Charlottenburg; Dr. D. Diederichsen of the Theater-sammlung, University of Hamburg; Dr. Robert Steinfeld of the Theaterwissenschaftliches Archiv, Munich and Berlin-Charlottenburg; Dr. Hermann Friehs of the Bavarian State Opera, Munich; V. M. Kleofass of the Theatermuseum Clara Ziegler-Stiftung, Munich; the Stadt-und-Universitäts-Bibliothek, Frankfurt-am-Main; Dr. Rolf Badenhausen of the Württembergisches Staatstheater, Stuttgart; and Dr. Carl Niessen, Institut für Theaterwissenschaft an der Universität Köln, Cologne.

Vienna data and pictures were provided by Hugo Burghauser, Desi Halban (Mrs. Edward von Saher) and her cousin, Princess Boncompagni, Fritzi Schlesinger, and Lacy L. Herrmann.

James G. Stahlman, publisher of the *Nashville Banner* and former president of the Inter-American Press Association, gave the author introductions to Rodrigo de Llano, director general of *Excelsior,* and Miguel Lanz Duret, president and general manager of the Compañía Periodística Nacional. Other material on Caruso's conquest of Mexico was supplied by Ernesto de Quesada, Jr., of the Sociedad Musical Daniel, and Alfonso Stoopen y de Alba. Dr. Frank Garcia Montes of Havana, to whom the author was referred by William H. Seltsam, documented pictorially the tenor's sole Cuban engagement.

Pictures and material, often nowhere else to be found, were kindly made available by: R. W. Boyd, Jr., and Dorothea Bourne of *Time,* Arthur R. Murphy, Jr., of *Life,* Nancy Hamilton, Paul H. Bonner, Jr., Mrs. Rogers Winter of the *Augusta (Ga.) Chronicle,* André Ross of Ross, Court & Co., Toronto, John Freestone and Canon H. J. Drummond, the leading Caruso authorities of England, Misses Mathilde and Frances Lina Weber, Winifred Sobie of *Newsweek,* Rosa Ponselle, Joseph S. Ietti, William D. Whalen, Captain James M. Alfonte, Thurber N. Wilkins, James Cagney, Emil Roth, Louis Hyman, Victor E. Barrett of the Manger Vanderbilt Hotel, Mrs. Percy S. Chandler, Mrs. Lee Cheney Jessup, and Mrs. L. C. Naff, manager emeritus of the Ryman Auditorium, Nashville.

Finally, the author hereby acknowledges with grateful appreciation his indebtedness to Frank Chapman, who was directly responsible for starting him on an organized study of Caruso; to Henry B. Sell whose idea this book was in the first place; to Adrian and Marisa Zorgniotti for help in translations, particularly Caruso's letter to his brother, and in many other ways; to Maynard Morris and Phyllis Jackson of Music Corporation of America; to John Secrist for more than the last word in discography; to Walter W. Price, Jr.; and to Bryan Holme, wise and skillful, patient and understanding.

INTRODUCTION

THIS IS THE FIRST BOOK ABOUT CARUSO BY SOMEBODY WHO NEVER HEARD HIM. WHAT GIVES me the right, you may well inquire. When I ask the same of myself I take refuge in a speech Laurence Olivier made when he opened the gardens around Henry Irving's statue in London.

"He died two years before I was born," Sir Laurence said of the first actor to attain the order of knighthood, "and yet I am as conscious of him as if I had served as a member of his company."

Long before I read those lines I knew in my small way the feeling. In a decade at the Metropolitan there has not been a day I have not sensed Caruso's presence as though he were still a member of the company.

To literally millions of people his name spelled grand opera. He exerted an inestimable influence on the taste of both sides of the footlights. Tenors will never stop trying to imitate him, and to say a young artist is "like Caruso" is more often a sentence rather than a compliment.

In less than a score of years in America he established the financial security of the two organizations he served—the Victor Talking Machine Company and the Metropolitan Opera; but his success in certain works like *Aida* and *Pagliacci* left its mark on the repertoire no less than it did on the receipts.

A generation after he had sung his last, Claudia Cassidy of the *Chicago Tribune* was to write, ". . . Caruso is as urgent in communication as if he had closed the door of a room, not of life."

The most ready proof of this is his record royalties which seem to defy the law of diminishing returns. The sums paid his estate since his death have been as great as they were in his lifetime. They show no sign of decline. But immortality is something more substantial than the columns of a balance sheet.

From all over the world visitors to the Metropolitan stand before the mammoth, laurel-crowned head, so like a Caesar and so unlike Caruso. On the red walls of the opera restaurant hangs a portrait of him in *La Juive,* looking more like a road company Shylock than the imposing Eléazar we know he must have been. The bas-relief on the parterre floor was unveiled the year after his death and Mrs. Caruso herself presented the big silver bust in the family circle foyer. The feeling of real presence, however, is not dependent on iconography.

Ask anyone the first time he heard the name of Caruso. The chances are he can no more tell you than he can recall his first awareness of George Washington or Shakespeare; but I well remember the first time I heard the voice of Caruso on a record. A lady had come to our school (the Victor Company had an "Educational Department" in those days) demonstrating the victrola in the fond hope that the school board or perhaps some well-to-do member of the Parent-Teachers might fall for one of the big quarter-sawed jobs with the morning-glory horn. How often I have wondered what became of that lady of the pince-nez, tailored suit and bird hat. Without my knowing it she gave me my first lesson in showmanship: Never play down to your audience.

She put on Caruso and Alda's record of the "Miserere" from *Trovatore*. She told us the story of the opera, a plot which to this day I would be hard put to unravel; but the picture she drew was quite clear. We had no trouble whatever visualizing the terror-stricken Leonora as her lover's voice rang out from the donjon tower. May I pause here to say this unforgettable impression suffered a severe jolt some years later when I heard the Metropolitan for the first time and the tenor jumped prison long enough to take several hearty bows in the middle of the act.

But a gong sounded in my head that morning more penetrating than the death knell which started the "Miserere." Aside from the sound of Caruso the strongest impression I carried away from that combined concert and sales pitch was our wonderful visitor's account of the fees which Caruso was rolling up in South America. I didn't need the figures to tell me the voice was 24-karat; nevertheless, they did not disturb the picture and they rang up an indelible entry in my brain. A boss of mine once said I always had my feet in the clouds and my head in the box office.

After that phonographic matinee the full-page ads of the Victor Company took on new meaning—Caruso as des Grieux, Farrar as Tosca, Galli-Curci as Gilda, and a host of others in resplendent color trooping out of a shiny mahogany phonograph under the Christmas tree ("Will these great artists sing in your home on Christmas morning?"); Caruso as Rhadames in a dugout (this one appeared in November 1918) standing beside a table model victrola fresh from the packing case. "Cheering our boys in France," was the caption of this rather extraordinary scene.

The closest he came to me in space was his only appearance in Nashville, sixty miles away. It was the day after my ninth birthday. I didn't even think about going to the concert. Such experiences were as remote from me in those days as the moon for which I might as well have asked. Anyway, Caruso was something that was going on forever, like Niagara Falls. My time would come.

One August afternoon a little more than two years later the front page of the *Nashville Banner* gave us the big shock. The Associated Press dispatch from Naples, including date and credit, ran only three lines. "Enrico Caruso," it read, "world-famous tenor, died here today." There were four paragraphs from London and a two-column follow from New York, both by the AP. How was it in a drowsy Tennessee town more than five thousand miles away I could feel such a wrench, such a personal loss for somebody I had never seen? It was a bright sunny day but suddenly the world was a duller place.

Two summers ago I visited Naples for the first time. I had been in Italy previously but now I was continuing a pilgrimage which had begun more than thirty years before and will last as long as I do—the quest of someone who missed hearing him, who felt sorely deprived and was trying to make up for it. To a degree I represent a whole generation of music-lovers. I have sought, am seeking, every place on record associated importantly with his life. I am finding others on my own.

Just as he rarely disappointed an audience by failure to appear, or, through some fault never his own, by giving less than his incomparable best, Caruso has never let me down. Do I go too far when I say that on my level my efforts are bound up with a resolve not to let him down? With Huneker I say ". . . he remains the dearest memory in this drab, prosaic age."

FRANCIS ROBINSON

New York
January 1957

CONTENTS

The story begins and ends here. Vesuvius at its most active was never a match for Naples on an ordinary day. Her roaring streets were Caruso's first home, the backdrop of his first appearances. In the great San Carlo Theater he had one of the few flops of his life—something he never forgave or forgot. Ironically and without realizing it, he came home to die.

CHAPTER I

BEGINNING

T HE HOUSE AT 7 VIA SAN GIOVANELLO AGLI OTTOCALLI APPEARS TO HAVE CHANGED LITTLE
in the past eighty years. Far from being a national monument, there is not so much as a plaque
to tell you that here is the birthplace of the greatest singer of his time, perhaps of all time.

The neighborhood is not the most ancient part of Naples. Compared with the jungle of right
angles in the old quarter, through which even a tiny Italian-made car can hardly pass without mow-
ing down a substantial percentage of the population, the street is light, airy and open. And it has the
luxury, however narrow, of sidewalks.

If the building has had a coat of paint since Enrico Caruso was born there all trace of it has
vanished. Two miserable shops with the inevitable neon signs mar the front of the ground floor.
Otherwise, the façade preserves that dignity of balance between mass and line which in Italy, more
than in any country on earth, is bestowed on the homes of rich and poor alike.

The courtyard is no filthier than many in New Orleans; nor is it any the more attractive because this happens to be Europe. But once in the room where the voice sounded for the first time,
something takes hold of you.

The sweet-faced tenant is courteous after the manner of most of her compatriots, the open
friendliness which is neither servility nor condescension. Yes, she tells you, this is the place. Eight
or ten children, cleaner than those in the street, swarm around the double bed which all but fills the
room.

What angel hovered over this room the morning of February 25, 1873? Thank God it was
not the dark one which visited the house most often in those years. Enrico Caruso was the eighteenth
of twenty-one children and the first to live past infancy.

You give a few lire to the beautiful children, who have been eying you as though you were a
visitor from another planet, and go back into the blinding sunlight. Although in photographs the
Church of SS. John and Paul next door is quite impressive, another example that dignity and beauty
in this land are no respecters of wealth and rank, it is probably the smallest house of public worship
in the world. In this tiny church Enrico was baptized—Errico, the parish register reads, which in
Neapolitan is to Enrico as Harry is to Henry in English. Enrico did not evolve until some years later.

The financial situation of the Caruso family, while never flush, was neither as dire as has been pictured. A good mechanic and a two-fisted drinker, Marcellino Caruso held a responsible job with the Meuricoffre factory which made cottonseed oil and purified cream of tartar. In time he moved up to superintendent of the establishment.

After Enrico there was another little boy "without the strength to live." Giovanni, the brother who survived him, was born in 1876 and, six years later, the only girl, Assunta.

There is no photograph of the child Caruso. To compensate for this you find yourself mentally pinning his face on every urchin you see. Usually it fits. Huneker says he was always a boy.

In one of his rare autobiographical moments, Caruso tells of lying in bed, the covers pulled over his head, while his mother and father had a violent argument as to his future. Marcellino was for putting him to work then and there. Anna demanded he go on with school. Anna won but it was she who had to find the tuition money, five lire (one dollar) a month.

Father Bronzetti, who ran a school at 33 via Postica Maddalena, had drilled his choir until it was one of the best in all the city, in demand on every religious holiday and at many private social functions in between.

While we are wishing, those of us who have never heard Caruso may just as well yearn to know what he was like as the finest boy contralto in Naples. He came to be known as "Carusiello" and "the little divo" and he began to misbehave accordingly. Once when he had sung the Mercadante Mass particularly well at Amalfi he refused to ride home inside the carriage with his teacher and the other boys. His place, he insisted, was on the box up with the coachman; and there he perched until he dropped off to sleep, came perilously near falling under the wheels, and was transferred bodily to safety below.

Such outbursts didn't go down at all well with Marcellino. In his second year at the Bronzetti Institute Carusiello took first prize. As he was returning to his place, the gold medal gleaming on his little chest, the deposed champion, identified by Caruso only as Pietro, sprang from his desk and attacked him. In the ensuing fight Caruso drew his assailant's blood. Instantly the spectators' sympathy swung to Pietro. Even Father Bronzetti took it upon himself to rebuke Enrico, whereupon the little divo tore his prize from his lapel and threw it at the principal's feet.

It was now Marcellino's turn to get into the act. A chunky, powerful man, he dealt a blow which his son never forgot. What followed was infinitely more painful. "Kneel down," he roared, "and kiss Father Bronzetti's feet."

"I vowed I would never sing for the Institute again," Caruso wrote years later, the sting of that humiliation still on him, "and this vow was kept sacred and inviolate." After a year, he left school and took a job in a mechanical laboratory.

Instinctively neat and orderly, he excelled at mechanical drawing and was quite aware of the value of his services. He was about twelve when he went in to his boss and asked for a raise. It was refused. Forthwith he quit and went to work for a manufacturer of drinking fountains.

On the feast of Corpus Christi, 1888, Anna Caruso lay seriously ill. Enrico did not want to sing but his mother insisted. With a heavy heart he trudged to the Church of San Severino. It was one of only two performances in his life he was unable to finish. In the middle of the service the weeping neighbors came to tell him his mother was gone.

"Out of regard for her," he said, "I had resigned myself to pursuing my work as a mechanic's apprentice. After her death, though my heart was filled with sadness over my irreparable loss, I could see no reason for continuing this sacrifice. I left the office never to return and decided to dedicate all to music."

Marcellino was furious at this turn of events. Being a mechanic had been good enough for him. Why wasn't it for his son? He ordered Enrico out of the house. "Was he simply threatening me?" Many years later Caruso still did not have the answer; but he did know he could no longer remain under his father's roof. To his credit he never held this against the old man. Indeed he was extremely close to the stepmother Marcellino provided, less than six months after poor Anna had been laid to rest.

For ten years the Carusos had been living at 54 via San Cosmo e Damiano. The organist in the nearby Church of Sant' Anna alle Paludi took in the sixteen-year-old boy and gave him (these are Caruso's words) "the joy of a first engagement." What wouldn't his admirers give to hear, just once, the litany he told of singing a hundred times for two lire—forty cents—at the long Tuesday services.

Every visitor to Naples remembers the public swimming places which line the Bay. At one of these, the Risorgimento Baths, Enrico did his first secular singing. In the summer of 1891, while playing the resort circuit, he met Eduardo Missiano, one of a sizable list of people who would be anonymous today had they not helped Caruso mount the ladder of fame. To Missiano must go the credit of being Caruso's real discoverer. Never forgetting an act of kindness, Caruso, when he came into his own, saw to it that his baritone friend was engaged for small roles at the Metropolitan.

Missiano's teacher, Vergine, was unimpressed by Caruso's voice; or at least he said he was. "It sounds," he remarked, "like the wind whistling through the windows." Another time he commented, "It is like gold at the bottom of the Tiber, hardly worth digging for." Nevertheless, he accepted him as a pupil and drew up a contract which Caruso eight years later had hell's own time getting out of: twenty-five per cent of all earnings for the first five years—and here is the joker— *of actual singing.*

At twenty, like every young Italian of the time, Caruso was greeted for military service. There was in the land neither war nor rumors of war, but Caruso was thrown into something akin to shock. His friends assured him he would be classified the nineteenth-century Italian equivalent of 4-F, but he passed the physical in a walk. Shortly after his twenty-first birthday, pale and trembling, he reported to the Thirteenth Artillery in Rieti.

As a soldier Caruso was a hopeless misfit, and his commanding officer, a certain Major Nagliotti, was the first to know it. More important, he was as quick to recognize Caruso the singer. Here is the story in the tenor's own words:

> One day, it was Easter, the battalion all dined together at a dinner given by the officers to the soldiers. Major Nagliotti presided at the head of the table. After the dessert, the soldiers, in unison, demanded that I sing the Brindisi from *Cavalleria Rusticana.* I sang it, was applauded and requested to give an encore. But Major Nagliotti rose and reproved everyone for insisting that I sing it again and above all rebuked me for not appreciating my gift. He said he felt obliged to assume the care of it and this he would do by jailing everyone who asked me to sing. He added that he would treat me in like manner should I accede to their demands. The rebuke restrained the enthusiasm instantly. A few days later, the respected major called me aside and besides favoring me with exemption from some of the difficult exercises he suggested that I retire from military service and substitute my brother in my place.

As to just how this extraordinary transfer was accomplished Caruso is silent, but poor Giovanni, perhaps as reluctantly, certainly no more inappropriately, suddenly found himself under arms. Like any of his able-bodied young countrymen, Enrico had a military life expectancy of three years. He was out in two months, but not before Nagliotti had done him another service. The major had brought him to a rich nobleman in the town who loved music and was a good pianist.

The baron was a kind man and enjoyed playing for the young recruit, painstakingly correcting his mistakes. On the piano was a score of *Cavalleria Rusticana* which had burst on the world in nearby Rome four years before. They went to work on it. In five days Caruso had learned the entire role of Turiddu. A year later this was to be his first part in standard opera—but that is another chapter.

Gloria Caruso

Gloria Caruso

Marcellino Caruso. Some of the strong will which was transmitted to the son shows in the father's face.

Anna Bardino Caruso. From a pastel of his adored mother which always stood on Caruso's bedside table.

Pasquale J. Simon

16

Pasquale J. Simonelli

The house at 7 via San Giovanello agli Ottocalli (opposite) has changed little in the past eighty years. There is no marker to tell you that in the tiny room with the balcony the world's greatest tenor was born. In the Church of SS. John and Paul, next door, he was baptized. When he was six the family moved to via San Cosmo e Damiano (above) and Enrico was sent to kindergarten for two years. Thereafter his formal education was scant.

Grassi

Via Postica Maddalena (below) was the site of Father Bronzetti's school where Enrico received his first instruction in music. In no time his beautiful contralto voice was in demand all over Naples and as far away as Amalfi. He came to be known as "the little divo." At left is the entrance to the Meuricoffre factory where Marcellino Caruso was a mechanic and later superintendent. Enrico himself was a clerk in the warehouse at sixteen.

Pasquale J. Simonelli

He was singing at the Church of San Severino (above) the night his mother died. If Marcellino had had his way Enrico might never have got past the factory, but Anna Caruso sensed what had been entrusted to her. She it was who squeezed out the monthly five lire for his lessons. At right is the fountain at the Bridge of Cerra he adjusted as a boy mechanic. He never failed to visit it on his return trips to Naples.

Pasquale J. Simonelli

Gloria Caruso

Caruso made his debut at twenty-one in *L'Amico Francesco,* an opera by a young man with more money than talent. Both composer and work are forgotten today except for Caruso's having touched them. The tenor received eighty lire (sixteen dollars) for the four scheduled performances. Poor *Francesco* survived only two, but Caruso had a success and the grateful composer gave him a bonus of fifty lire. The Teatro Nuovo where all this took place burned but was rebuilt on the site (above) and is now a movie house. Note the two young fans devouring the poster. Left, Caruso at eighteen. Opposite, the famous first published photograph. There is reason for the classic drapery. When the photographer arrived Caruso's only shirt had gone to the laundry and a bedspread was pressed into service.

20

He was twenty-two and thin as an anchovy when he made his start in standard opera with *Cavalleria Rusticana* at the Cimarosa Theater in Caserta. A music-loving baron had taught him the role the year before when he was doing a stretch in the army. It was to become one of his great parts. Here are three big moments from that 1895 debut. At left, Turiddu reviles Santuzza. The soprano is Elena Bianchini-Cappelli who later in the same year sang *Manon Lescaut* with Caruso in Egypt. At right is the famous drinking song. Above, Turiddu's farewell to his mother.

Pasquale J. Simonelli

24

Giacinto Prandelli

Even before *L'Amico Francesco,* Caruso auditioned for the Mercadante Theater (opposite) in Naples and failed abysmally. That bad memory was erased in 1895-96. He was called on several times to sing there twice in the same day—*Traviata* in the afternoon and *Rigoletto* at night. On such occasions the manager was known to lock him in the dressing room between shows and hoist him his dinner of sardine and cream cheese sandwiches by hook and line. The following year Caruso triumphed at the Massimo Theater, Palermo, (above) despite the Sicilians' resentment of "foreign" talent. At right, Caruso in 1896.

25

La Favorita at the Mercadante, 1895. Here is Fernando, a young novice who forsakes the monastery because of a beautiful girl he has seen. He returns to the cloister when he finds his beloved is the mistress of the King of Castile for whom he has won honors in battle. This makes sense when you listen to Caruso's record of the last act aria.

Gloria Ca[...]

A town that lives forever in the memory of Americans. On this Salerno poster Caruso was still known, Neapolitan style, as Errico. Enrico did not emerge until some time later. He cracked his high notes regularly but to the everlasting credit of the Salerno public a few troublesome top notes in such a voice did not matter. Lombardi, his teacher, was the impresario.

At twenty-three in Trapani, the only audience on record to see him under the influence of alcohol. He drank no more than usual but he had no previous experience with Sicilian wine. The voice came all right but he tangled with some of the lyrics of *Lucia* and barely escaped lynching. Once, however, the audience had sampled the replacement it immediately demanded Caruso's return.

Edward Johnson

Caruso had only two singing teachers, Vergine and Vincenzo Lombardi (above). It was Lombardi who came to Caruso's rescue when the B-flat kept breaking. He was also the teacher of Edward Johnson.

Gloria Caruso

At Salerno in 1896 Caruso first undertook the role he was to make forever his own, the tragic clown in *Pagliacci*. He established the popularity of the work at the Metropolitan, and *Vesti la giubba* virtually became his signature. Irving Kolodin says, ". . . almost every audience believes that any tenor who dons the costume of Canio, beats a drum, and makes loud vocal noises is affording a reasonably close approximation of Caruso."

28

Caruso's deep friendship with Giuseppe De Luca dates from their days in Genoa. They lived in the same pension and used to race each other through the Galleria for coffee. Caruso was beginning to put on weight and more often than not was the loser. Opposite, they are shown in *The Pearl Fishers* in 1898. Eighteen years later they opened the season at the Metropolitan together in the same opera.

Above is Genoa's beautiful Carlo Felice Theater, which was bombed during World War II and for a time gave performances in a roofless shell. At right, Caruso is seen in Leoncavallo's *La Bohème*. Although written at the same time as Puccini's *Bohème,* this work was not produced until fifteen months later and never gained wide success. Leoncavallo makes his tenor the painter, Marcello, instead of the poet.

The pictures of Caruso on these two pages are from the tenor's Roman period. His first appearance at the Costanzi Theater (above), later known as the Teatro Reale and now as the Teatro dell' Opera, was as Osaka in Mascagni's *Iris* (left). He later sang the part in Buenos Aires and New York. *Iris* has not been heard at the Metropolitan since 1931 when Rethberg, Gigli, De Luca, and Pinza performed the roles taken in 1907 by Eames, Caruso, Scotti, and Journet and in 1915 by Bori, Botta, Scotti again, and Didur, Toscanini conducting. Osaka's serenade of Jor, the son of the sun, which helps lure Iris off to the geisha house, sounds suspiciously like the *Siciliana* from *Cavalleria,* but the work has moments of real beauty and charm, notably the soprano's two arias and the *Hymn to the Sun* which opens and closes the fantasy.

In Rome Caruso suffered one of the major disappointments of his career. He had been told that to him would fall the honor of creating the tenor lead in *Tosca,* which appropriately enough had its première in Rome, where the action takes place. Just why Puccini withdrew the coveted opportunity has never been explained, but Caruso did not complain and he and the composer became fast friends. "One's career is neither so brilliant nor so easy as may seem to the casual eyes of the public," was Caruso's laconic comment on the incident. The last time he sang in Rome was at a benefit in 1914 to help get Italian workingmen out of Germany.

M. Dosio & C.

The history of music is full of sopranos who marry their singing teachers. Less prevalent, but still frequent, is the young male singer who is helped along by an older prima donna. When Caruso sang *La Bohème* at Leghorn in 1897 the Mimi was Ada Giachetti. It was love at first sight, but she was married and there is no divorce in Italy. The two lived together until she deserted him eleven years later. Of the four children she bore him, two survived, Rodolfo, named for the poet in *Bohème* and called Fofò, and Enrico, Jr., nicknamed Mimmi, again after Puccini. Caruso loved his sons, publicly acknowledged them and legally gave them his name.

Franco Colom

Caruso's Milan debut was not at La Scala but at the Lirico (opposite page) where he learned *La Navarraise* in five days. He sang in the première of *L'Arlesiana* there November 27, 1897, and in the *Lament* of Federico the true Caruso voice may have been disclosed for the first time. A year later Giordano selected him to create the tenor lead in *Fedora*. After that night his name flashed across the entire operatic world. "The contracts descended on me like a heavy rainstorm," Caruso candidly recorded. In Milan, Caruso and his family lived at 1 via Velasca, the doorway of which is shown at right.

Marziale Sisca

Caruso with his two sons, Fofò and Mimmi.

The Lirico is now a vaudeville theater.

Nicola Valente

A. Lorens

One of the offers which came to Caruso after the *Fedora* première was from Russia. Because of the high fees and the prestige involved this was the next engagement he accepted. His St. Petersburg bow was in *La Bohème.* The photograph of him as Rodolfo at left was made there at the time, December 1898. Russia heard his first *Aida.* Caruso's name is third from the top in the cast of characters of the program illustrated on this page. On February 15, 1899, he sang *Cavalleria Rusticana,* followed by three acts of *Lucia,* the handbill (opposite page) announcing that the evening would conclude with the *Mad Scene.* Tetrazzini sang the title role. The name of Battistini was also on this impressive roster and the repertoire further included *Pagliacci; Maria di Rohan,* an old Battistini warhorse; and *Traviata,* with Tetrazzini of course. At the world première of *Traviata* a 300-pound prima donna sent the audience into howls of laughter when she announced she was wasting away with consumption. Only her divine voice spared Tetrazzini a similar fate. There was a concert at the Imperial Palace after which the Czar presented Caruso with a pair of gold cuff links set with diamonds. The tenor describes the ill-fated monarch as a "small, almost insignificant-looking man with an anxious face."

Caruso was invited back to St. Petersburg
the following year and in March of 1900
moved on to the Bolshoi Theater, Moscow,
(right), adding *Faust* to the repertoire he
had sung in the capital—*Aida, Mefistofele,*
and *A Masked Ball.*

Luisa Tetrazzini in *Lucia.*

ИТАЛЬЯНСКАЯ ОПЕРА
подъ упр. Г. АНТОНІО УГЕТТИ.
ВЪ БОЛЬШОМЪ ЗАЛѢ СПБ. КОНСЕРВАТОРІИ
ИМПЕРАТОРСКАГО
РУССКАГО МУЗЫКАЛЬНАГО ОБЩЕСТВА
Въ Понедѣльникъ, 15-го Февраля, въ 8 час. веч.
Дано будетъ для **девятаго** спектакля **перваго** абонемента:
I. СЕЛЬСКАЯ ЧЕСТЬ
Опера въ 1-мъ актѣ, музыка Масканьи.
Участвующіе: Г-жи Тильде Каротини, Паганелли;
Гг. Энрико Каруссо, Витторіо Бромбара и др.
II. ЛЮЧІА
Опера въ 3-хъ актахъ, музыка Доницетти.
(Опера оканчивается сценою сумасшествія въ 3-мъ актѣ).
Участв.: Г-жа Луиза Тетрацини; Гг. Энрико Каруссо,
Витторіо Бромбара, Алессандро Сильвестри и др.
Соло на арфѣ исполнитъ солистка Итальянской оперы
Г-жа Кине-Вальтеръ.

Ministry of Culture, U. S. S. R.

Another Russian photograph as Rodolfo. Note Caruso uses the Italian Pietroburgo for St. Petersburg, but his name is signed in Russian characters, a revealing touch. As courteous a man as ever lived, he liked to address others each in his own tongue. He was also aware of the world about him and eager to learn. Laid end to end his schooling would not have added up to a year, but he got along in seven languages, sang in four. He swore he could detect no difference between *des yeux* and *des cieux,* yet he learned the difference and came to sing French, especially *Faust,* remarkably well.

The world première of *Tosca* was January 14, 1900. Before the year was out Caruso got his chance at Cavaradossi—twelve performances at Treviso between October 23 and November 11 with Ada Giachetti in the title role. The sacristan is Ettore Borelli. The conductor was Egisto Tango, who had a season at the Metropolitan, 1909-10, and was on the podium for several notable *Toscas,* the most memorable of which must have been December 11 with Caruso and Fremstad. Puccini heard Caruso do the part in Bologna and had to admit he had never heard the music better sung.

G. Ferretto

13.1.11. Via Verdi, 4,
Milano

Caro Caruso

Vado al verde Tordellag
colla neve che c'è a Milfa
non c'è mezzo di restar
Ho nel cuor, nell'alma l'ec
della voce tua divina
Ci vedremo quanto pri
nella Roma un pò papa
E Missiano a voce Turca
e il fratello molto nero
ed il Conte col sombrero
stanno bene di salu?
Segurola in vetro antic
colla voce rotondetta
io ti prego in tutta fretta
salutarmi insieme a Lor
Là dall'oste Don Gennaro

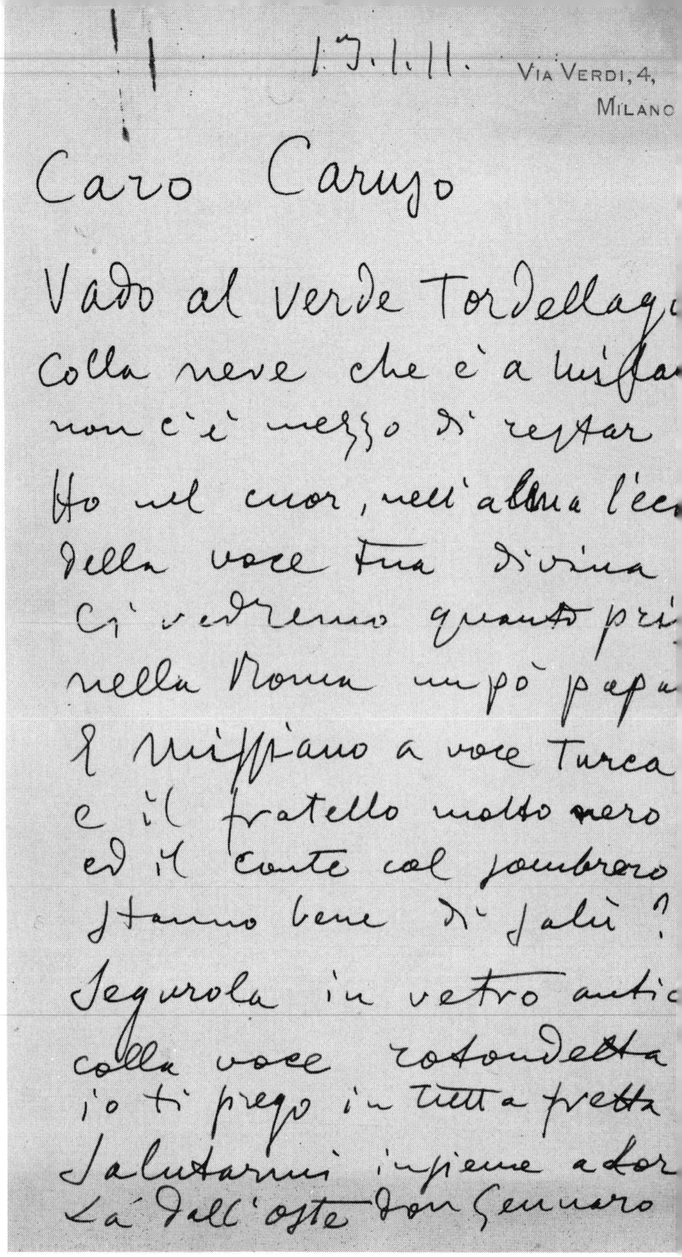

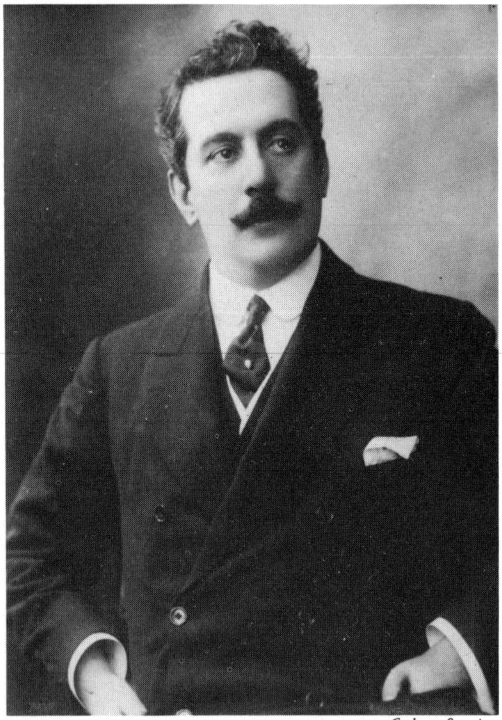

Puccini.

Culver Service

Puccini settled at Torre del Lago because he liked duck shooting, and the landscape was dear to his Tuscan heart. Note the swivel chair in his study which serves both desk and piano and the position of all three with relation to the door. Puccini used to begin work in full hunting regalia. If he sighted a likely quarry over the lake poor *Butterfly* was left to languish on the music rack. In this very room Caruso sang for the master before he got the *Bohème* engagement in Leghorn. The warmth of their friendship is attested by the letter (above) written soon after the première of *The Girl of the Golden West.* "Dear Enrico," the second half reads in part, "be careful not to fall into the net. Tell me how *Fanciulla* is doing and if the crowds are flocking to it and if it is paying me well. . . . I salute you, O singer of many notes, and hope that the cheek of a *fanciulla* will repose on your breast. . . . A kiss to my Rodolfo and my extraordinary Johnson from him who wishes well to Rhadames.

"Good-bye, your
"PUCCINI."

mangerete giocherete
Caro Enrico sta un po' attento
non cadere nella rete –
dimmi come la Fanciulla
fra denari e folla folta
mi rispondi? mi fai pago
scrivi pure a Torre del Lago
Ti saluto senza punto
o cantor di tante note
che le Tonde e grasse gote
di fanciulle anche ostrogole
Ti si pospin sul tuo sen-
ciccin al Tondo compilato
o Renà Radolfo e Mari.
o mio Johnson straordinario
prendi un bacio da colui
che t'istima e ti vuol bene
e ti stringe bene bene
quella man dista Radames
ciao tuo Puccini

Gloria Caruso

Puccini's study.

Museo Teatrale, Teatro alla Scala

La Scala, shrine of Italian opera for nearly two hundred years.

The Verdi commemoration program.

Caruso's first appearance at La Scala (in *La Bohème*) was, in the words of the general manager, Giulio Gatti-Casazza, "not lucky." He was suffering from laryngitis and sang at a personal sacrifice to avert a postponement. A new work of Mascagni failed but Caruso had a success, the more creditable since he had to carry a flop. The best, however, was to come. In *L'Elisir d'Amore* with Toscanini conducting he scored a triumph which, according to Mr. Gatti, "remained a sensation in the annals of the Teatro alla Scala." On January 27, 1901, one month and a day after Caruso's debut at La Scala, "the heartbeat of Italy stopped for an instant." Giuseppe Verdi died at the age of eighty-eight. At the Scala where the old man had had his share of triumph and failure there was a solemn commemoration conducted by Toscanini. Caruso sang the tenor in the *Rigoletto* Quartet. His skill as a draftsman—caricaturist in this instance is hardly the word —was never more evident than in the drawing of Verdi below.

Marziale Sisca

A Boldini portrait of Verdi hangs in the House of Repose for Musicians in Milan.

Caruso had an agreement with Maurice Grau for New York but Grau dawdled, possibly because he was ill and on the way out as impresario at the Metropolitan. In the letter below there is some sharp talk about fees which shows our hero was no mean business man. The last paragraph reads: "It also seems to me that Mr. Grau does not have artists of great payment (i.e. high-salaried) which is absurd since one must understand that I also take a risk in coming to America and one does not move himself for nothing. In any event if this does not suit Mr. Grau it is of little importance because I prefer to make contracts without strangulation clauses rather than those with articles of death and a lot of money."

GRAND HÔTEL MILAN

SALSOMAGGIORE - TERME

10/9/902

Egregio Sig Fano

Milano

Dopo il vostro telegram-
ma come vedete scrivo subi
to e mando i contratti for
mati ma però nel modo
come dissi nel mio tele
gramma di stamani.
Bisogna che faccia
te notare al Sig Grau che
per l'America del Sud

i danari anticipati sono
stati e saranno uguali
quelli che lui ha anzi
di più perchè l'anno s
so ricevetti in anticipo
Trentacinquemila e q
to venturo anno saran
no Quarantacinquem
e i Sigg. Nardi e Boul
ti non hanno messo n
contratto il sesto arti
lo del Sig Grau.
Poi mi sembra che
il Sig Grau non abb

Reginald Allen

avuti degli artisti di gran
de paga, ciò che è assur
do, dappoichè bisogna capi
re che anche io rischio
per andare in America
e per niente nessuno
si muove. Del resto
poi se al sig° Grau
non andasse ciò a
me mi fa poco perchè
preferisco più fare con
tratti senza articoli di
morte che quelli con lo
morte e molti Hanari
Salutandovi dto
Enrico Caruso

The South American *Lohengrin* (see program) was Caruso's only public venture into the German repertoire. Had he lived, who can say? Old subscribers at the Metropolitan tell how he used to slip in the back of the house and stand for Urlus' *Tristan*. Among the scores Mrs. Caruso gave the Peabody Institute Library in Baltimore are songs of Schubert and Schumann, the *Prize Song* from *Meistersinger* and the aria from *Rosenkavalier* in German with his markings, which shows he must have studied them in the original language. In Hamburg he was offered the role of the Singer in *Der Rosenkavalier* but the budget was not sufficient to cover his fee. The most eloquent testimony is that of Huneker, the distinguished critic of the *Times* and later the *World:* "Once for my delectation he hummed the plaintive measures of the dying Tristan. Tears came to my eyes, so penetratingly sweet was his tone, so pathetic his phrasing."

George Siegel

"As the Yankees and the Dodgers split Americans into rival camps," observes Herbert Kubly in *American in Italy,* "La Scala and San Carlo divide Italians." Caruso had two strikes against him the night of December 30, 1901, when he made his San Carlo debut: first, the Neapolitans were probably suspicious of his *L'Elisir d'Amore* on which La Scala had so lavishly bestowed its approval, and second, human nature being what it is, he was probably the prophet without honor in his own country. In any event, to this day habitués of San Carlo (left) take a perverse delight in pointing out that Caruso "was hissed here," one of only three theaters in the world to enjoy this doubtful distinction, the others being the Opera in Budapest (below) and the Liceo in Barcelona.

István Molnár, Legation of the Hungarian People's Republic, Washington

This picture of the house in via Foria where Caruso installed his father and stepmother and where Marcellino died serves well to symbolize the tenor's break with his home city and virtually the rest of Italy. Booing is a sound an artist never gets over. To sensitive ears it is more terrible than the screaming of a bomb or the bursting of a shell. Very rarely did Caruso sing in his homeland again, and, professionally, he shook the dust of Naples from his boots forever. "I will never again come to Naples to sing," he vowed; "it will be only to eat a plate of spaghetti."

CHAPTER II

THE CAREER

"ALONG CRESCENDO" IS THE WAY A *New York Times* HEADLINE DESCRIBED CARUSO'S CA-
reer, a summation so true and appropriate it points up the three harsh discords which
crashed amid the chorus of praise.

After alternately cheering and hissing, Barcelona let him finish his 1904 debut there in stony
silence. Budapest whistled him in 1907. He never returned to either place. But the cruelest blow he
suffered was the first, in 1901, when the audience in all the world he wanted most to please denied
him, the great San Carlo Theater in Naples. Many a time as a boy he must have passed the beautiful
old house and dreamed of singing there.

The very fact that he had a success at La Scala under his belt worked against him in the city of
his birth. He had also declined to pay his respects to the *sicofanti,* an incredible bunch of phonies
led by a self-appointed tribunal of effete noblemen and journalists.

Once he had delivered, however, the public, including his initial detractors, tried to make up
to him. They did not know their man. He played out the remaining nine performances of his contract magnificently but with cold disdain. He never appeared before a Neapolitan audience again.

His entry in the official history of the Teatro di San Carlo is a meager four lines:

"ENRICO CARUSO. Singing son of singing Naples. Nearly all his splendid career was spent in
America where he created, among other operas, *The Girl of the Golden West* at the Metropolitan
in New York. He sang at San Carlo in 1905 in *L'Elisir d'Amore* and *Manon.* After that he did not
wish to sing in Naples . . ."

The three dots as well as the incorrect date are the San Carlo historian's. What an epitaph for
Naples' most famous son.

With the less pretentious public of his home town Caruso had been a different story. His first
appearance on any stage was at the Teatro Nuovo seven years before and even in that modest frame-
work he scored a success.

Not long out of the army, he was offered the leading role in a little piece called *L'Amico
Francesco* by Mario Morelli, a wealthy and untalented amateur. *Francesco* had only two perform-

Opposite: The Metropolitan, for seventy-five years "the goal of every
opera singer from the Volga to the Hudson." From his debut there
November 23, 1903, until his death it was Caruso's artistic home.

Seligman

ances, but at one of the intermissions the impresario of the Cimarosa Theater in Caserta wandered back with a contract for the following April. His debut was in *Cavalleria Rusticana* just a year after he learned it from the kindly baron in Rieti.

Business at the box office was not so good in Caserta that spring. Every morning Caruso had to ask the harassed impresario for his ten-lire cachet from the night before. Ultimately, the season was cut short and Enrico landed back in Naples with twelve cents in his pocket. "I was often hungry," Caruso once said of his youth, "but never unhappy."

Cairo beckoned next; not the famous opera house for the opening of which Verdi had written *Aida,* but a kind of resort spot called the Ezbekieh Gardens. After the Egyptian engagement he was tapped by the Bellini and then the Mercadante Theater in Naples.

At Salerno the conductor was Vincenzo Lombardi, Caruso's only other teacher. In Vergine's class Enrico had been known as "a glass voice" because he broke so easily. Every time he attacked the B-flat in the "Flower Song" from *Carmen* it split wide open. Lombardi came to the rescue. A man may not add a cubit to his stature, but Caruso by sheer determination built a top to his voice.

He was only twenty-five when he was catapulted into world fame by creating the tenor lead in the world première of *Fedora,* but this was the Teatro Lirico, Milan's second theater, and not La Scala. It did not matter. The news of his success went round the world. Offers poured in, from Russia and South America, from La Scala itself.

Late in 1899 Caruso had agreed with Maurice Grau to come to the Metropolitan at $200 a week for twenty weeks. There was a fifteen-day grace period. It stretched on into two months during which Mr. Grau disappeared. The impresario, it turned out, was at Karlsbad nursing the gout. He could not be reached. Caruso signed to return to St. Petersburg. "I've waited long enough," he sputtered to Grau's Italian agent. "I must have a new overcoat for the winter and some coal for my fireplace."

The next contract was for fifty performances a season at $1,000 each—five years with annual increases. Before this contract could take effect illness forced Grau's retirement. To his successor, Heinrich Conried, fell the honor of presenting Caruso for the first time in the United States.

Triumphal European engagements continued—London, Paris, Berlin, Vienna—until the outbreak of the war, but after his New York debut, November 23, 1903, the Metropolitan was Caruso's artistic home. In eighteen seasons there he sang 607 times in thirty-seven different operas.

Oddly enough, he did not create an immediate furor with either the press or the public. The critics complained of "his tiresome Italian affectations" and pined for Jean de Reszke. A month after he arrived, long enough for him to have caught on, there was a *Traviata* with Madame Sembrich, Caruso, and Scotti. The *Sun* next day noted the performance had been heard by "a small and apathetic audience" but did go on to say that Caruso "sang his music beautifully and succeeded in evoking warm applause which was hard to get last night."

About this time Caruso was becoming involved in something which at the start hardly anybody took seriously but which was to bring him his greatest rewards in fame as well as money. He had just participated in another world première, *Germania,* when F. W. Gaisberg of the Gramophone and Typewriter Company arrived in Milan and set up shop in the Grand Hotel, directly above the suite where Verdi had died the year before. The proposition relayed to London was for ten arias, to be done in a single afternoon, at a fee of one hundred pounds for the lot—about fifty dollars a record. London cabled back, "Fee exorbitant. Forbid you to record."

Mainly because he was too embarrassed to go back to Caruso with such an answer, Gaisberg took matters in his own hands and ordered the recording session to proceed. Caruso sauntered in, tossed off his ten numbers in two hours—without blemish, Gaisberg says—and was on his way.

The precious waxes were rushed to Hanover; the finished products reached London in time for release to coincide with Caruso's Covent Garden debut. They were a sensation. The Victor Talking Machine Company took over the G. and T. masters and also Caruso. His first records in this country were made less than three months after his Metropolitan debut, his last within a year of his death.

During his lifetime the Victor Company paid him $1,825,000, about $130,000 more than his earnings at the Metropolitan. Since his death his estate has reaped another near $2,000,000 in royalties from his records.

There are two stories as to how his final fee per performance at the Metropolitan was arrived at. His last contract is said to have been handed him with a blank space for the figure, but it had been whispered to Caruso that the board was prepared to go as high as $4,000.

"I don't think there is a singer in this world who in one performance can give more than twenty-five hundred dollars' worth of singing," Caruso is said to have replied. "If I ask for one cent more than twenty-five hundred dollars the public, one way or another, will find out and want from me that one cent more of singing which I have not got. Therefore, leave matters as they are, with only one difference; instead of giving me one first-class cabin from Italy to America and back, put down what they call today cabin de luxe."

The other came to light in the obituaries of Gatti-Casazza, who ruled the Metropolitan with an iron hand for twenty-seven years. Caruso came to the general manager's office with the news that he had been offered five thousand dollars a night by Hammerstein, who was giving the Met a run for its money and finally had to be paid to leave town.

"If you wish five thousand dollars we shall have to give it to you," Mr. Gatti is reported to have answered more in sorrow than in anger. "We will never let our Caruso go. Of course, we shall have to put second-rate singers in your cast. We shall hire a poor conductor and underpay him. We shall have to save on others to pay you. But we will pay you."

Caruso's face reddened. "I insist," he shouted, "that you pay me only twenty-five hundred!"

Such were the rewards. What about the penalties? Smothered by well-meant admiration on one side, he was beset all the days of his greatness by those who envied that greatness or who sought to take advantage of him. Reports that he had lost his voice circulated on regular schedule, but he probably suffered more from the admiration he excited than from the envy. He could never appear in public without involuntarily inciting a riot. Souvenir hunters, hero-worshipers, cranks, and interviewers haunted him. I am quoting a newspaper on this last.

But the battle which he had to fight alone was the hardest of all. "I never step on the stage," he once said, "without asking myself whether I will succeed in finishing the opera." In this very element of doubt—this compulsion to be everything or nothing, his merciless demands on himself, his relentless self-appraisal—lay so much of his greatness.

"Work, work, and again work," was his answer when asked his rule of success. Another time he said, "This is how I have succeeded. I never refused an engagement and I have never been without work with the exception of two months in Naples after my second engagement. . . .

"I never refused to work. If one would come to me and say, 'Will you go to such and such a place for the summer and sing?' I would ask 'How much will you pay me?' The answer is 'Two thousand dollars.' But I say, 'The price for that was three thousand.' 'Never mind,' they say, 'two thousand dollars is all that can be paid this summer,' and I refuse. 'Very well,' they say, 'we get so-and-so.' Then I make quick thoughts in my head"—describing swift geometric patterns on his brow—"and I say, 'I will go.' Otherwise I lose the summer and the experience. And the experience is everything."

When I am asked, as I often am, what has Caruso to say for today, I cite the above. In my time I have known at least six young tenors endowed with as much voice as Caruso had—when he started.

A reviewer of Mrs. Caruso's beautiful book, written twenty-four years after his death, knowingly summed it up:

"The source of his existence lay only in himself. This was true in every aspect of his life. . . . All in all he was himself the great work of art, the masterpiece."

Rigoletto was the opera of Caruso's New York, London, Paris, Berlin, and Vienna debuts. The role of the Duke of Mantua fitted him like a glove. No one before or since has tossed off *La donna è mobile* with such abandon. *Questa o quella* was the first record he made for the Victor company. He recorded the *Quartet* no less than four times with a string of sopranos it makes one dizzy to enumerate: Bessie Abott, Marcella Sembrich, Luisa Tetrazzini, and Amelita Galli-Curci. At Covent Garden his Gildas were Melba and, as she was later in Vienna, Selma Kurz.

Arthur F. Vesper

Metropolitan Opera House
Lessee - CONRIED METROPOLITAN OPERA CO.

GRAND OPERA
SEASON 1903-1904,
UNDER THE DIRECTION OF
MR. HEINRICH CONRIED.

OPENING NIGHT
MONDAY EVENING, NOVEMBER 23rd, 1903,
at 8 o'clock,

RIGOLETTO
OPERA IN FOUR ACTS.
MUSIC by VERDI.
Book by F. M. Piave.
(IN ITALIAN.)

GILDA ....MME. SEMBRICH
MADDALENA...............MME. LOUISE HOMER
GIOVANNA ....MISS BAUERMEISTER
LA CONTESSA..............MME. HELEN MAPLESON
UN PAGGIO......................MISS PÖRNSEN

IL DUCA.... ....MR. CARUSO
(His first appearance in this country.)
RIGOLETTO.......................MR. SCOTTI

SPARAFUCILE ....MR. JOURNET
MARULLO ....MR. BÉGUÉ
MONTERONE ....MR. DUFRICHE
BORSA.........................MR. MASIERO
CONTE di CEPRANO.............MR. CERNUSCO
USCIERE.........................MR. FANELLI

CONDUCTOR...................MR. ARTURO VIGNA
(His first appearance in this country.)

STAGE DIRECTOR...........MR. KARL SCHROEDER

SYNOPSIS OF SCENERY.
ACT I.—Hall in the Duke's Palace, Mantua.
ACT II.—The House of Rigoletto.
ACT III.—A Room in the Duke's Palace.
ACT IV.—The House of Sparafucile.
In ACT I., Divertissement by the Corps de Ballet.

50

An early Rhadames . . .

an unretouched one . . .

Alexander Eddy

and the majestic finished product.

Frank Garcia Montes

A. Bert

52

Just as he established the popularity of *Pagliacci*, Caruso is responsible for the place of *Aida* in the repertoire, by far the most frequently performed opera at the Metropolitan (well on the way to its 500th time) and the work which has had more opening nights there than any other. In the fifteen years before Caruso came, *Aida* had been sung forty-six times, or about three times a season. In the sixteen years Caruso did Rhadames it was given 110 times, of which Caruso sang sixty-four. Above is the great Consecration Scene as staged at the Metropolitan prior to the Bing regime. Caruso is the left of the two figures slightly in front of the chorus.

Heinrich Conried, who brought Caruso to New York.

Caruso's success in Puccini's works was no less solid in New York than it had been in Italy. At right, the heart-broken Rodolfo. He was not always so lachrymose in *Bohème,* the artist's garret providing him with excellent opportunities for the pranks he sometimes delighted in playing on his colleagues. Marcello, going out to buy medicine for the dying Mimi, once found the sleeves of his overcoat sewed up; another time Colline's stovepipe hat had been thoughtfully filled with water. One night in Philadelphia, Caruso sang the bass aria in the last act when de Segurola lost his voice. Nobody in the audience knew the difference.

Puccini, as noted, had already given his blessing to Caruso in *Tosca* but the composer's first night in New York was also the first Metropolitan performance of *Manon Lescaut.* The boat was late and Puccini went straight from the pier to the director's box. "Caruso," he reported, "was amazing." Four days later during rehearsals for the first *Butterfly* at the Metropolitan he wrote friends, "Caruso is singing like a god." The first Puccini Manon at the Metropolitan was Lina Cavalieri, (left) the first Butterfly Geraldine Farrar, both 1907. Caruso created the tenor lead in the world première of *The Girl of the Golden* West, more of which later.

The device of a play within a play is almost as old as the drama itself. In fact, when *Pagliacci* was introduced to Brussels a French playwright came forward with a plagiarism suit. Leoncavallo, however, had a clear defense. As a child he had heard a case tried in his father's court of a jealous actor who killed his wife following a performance. After conviction the actor was asked if he felt penitent. "I repent nothing!" he shouted in a voice which shook the courtroom. "On the contrary, if it were to do over I would kill her again!" Of such stuff is *Pagliacci* made.

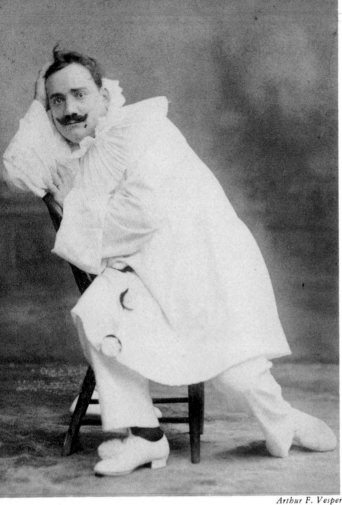

Pagliacci came back into real life on a May night in London in 1908. Caruso had suffered a severe blow during the voyage from America when the wireless brought word of his father's death. When he reached London he was greeted with the news that Ada Giachetti had left him. The next night he had to sing in the Albert Hall—Canio's *Lament,* "Laugh then, Pagliaccio, for your love that is shattered! Laugh for the pain that now has poisoned your heart!" The house went wild. Only Paolo Tosti and one other friend knew what was really going on behind the white mask.

Pagliacci reached the stage in 1892. Ten years later Leoncavallo wrote *Mattinata* "expressly for the Gramophone." He couldn't have guessed how "expressly," since half a century later it became the scourge of the juke boxes. With Leoncavallo himself at the piano, it was one of Caruso's first records. Caruso's attainments as an actor probably reached their height in *Pagliacci.* In the beginning his acting had been pronounced "awful." His figure was not meant for tragedy. But all this he overcame by the power and conviction of his performances. A man who by sheer will builds a top to his voice can do anything.

"The comedy is ended." Caruso gasps the last line of *Pagliacci* at the Metropolitan (above). *Pagliacci* with Caruso is the earliest operatic broadcast on record. In contrast to the millions who hear the Saturday matinees throughout the season today, the audience was a mere handful of persons. On the evening of January 13, 1910, Lee De Forest transmitted a portion of the performance from the stage of the Metropolitan to his coworkers in New Jersey and a few listeners huddled in Mr. Gatti's office.

Robert Lynn Batts Tobin

A hitherto unpublished self-caricature from Caruso's Vienna days.

Dr. Dulcamara (Didur) expounding the virtues of his magic elixir. When Caruso sang *Una furtiva lagrima* in the historic 1901 La Scala production of *L'Elisir d'Amore* it created such a furor he had to repeat it. The same thing happened three years later in his first season at the Metropolitan. By 1916 there was a house rule against encores. *L'Elisir* was a favorite for the last few years of his life. That he continued to sing the lyric roles of his youth along with his heroic parts was, in the words of Otto H. Kahn, "a most astounding artistic feat."

As Edgar of Ravenswood, Caruso donned plaids. Today the only kilted characters in *Lucia* at the Metropolitan are the dancers in the delightful ballet which opens the third act. Caruso sang *Lucia* with Galli-Curci in South America and made records with her here, but they never appeared together on the stage in the United States. Galli-Curci did not come to the Metropolitan until the season after his death.

With Frieda Hempel in *L'Elisir d'Amore.*

It was in *L'Elisir,* his only comic opera, that Caruso began to spit blood on the stage of the Brooklyn Academy of Music, December 11, 1920. "At that very moment," Gatti-Casazza, the general manager, wrote years later, "I had a fleeting premonition that Caruso was lost. It was the only time in my entire career as an opera director that I was obliged to end a performance in the middle."

59

Farrar Collection, Library of Congress

Geraldine Farrar first sang with Caruso in Monte Carlo. The tenor did not use full voice at rehearsals and when, at the performance, the full impact of Caruso hit her, Miss Farrar recalls, "I was literally stricken dumb with amazement and admiration . . . until the conductor, Vigna, rapped sharply with his baton to bring me back to my senses."

The Théatre Sarah Bernhardt was the scene of Caruso's first Paris appearances. Five years later came the Metropolitan season at the Châtelet across the way, the only European engagement in the company's history. In order to get a ticket for a Caruso opera, *Aida, Pagliacci,* or *Manon Lescaut,* the customer had to buy one for *Otello* or *Falstaff* in which he did not appear.

Serge Lido

Caruso's Berlin debut, October 5, 1904, was at the Theater des Westens, now the Städtische Oper. When the Kaiser invited him to Potsdam, Caruso insisted that his valet, Martino, be allowed to come along. After dinner the Kaiser raised his glass. "If I were not Emperor of Germany," he declared, "I should like to be Martino."

Aufnahme der Landesbildstelle Berlin

In Berlin Caruso also sang at the Royal Opera House, Unter den Linden, shown in the background of this cartoon. "A French plot," the caption reads. ("The Battle of the Opera House.") "All right, agreed, dear Caruso," says the French officer. "This year you will make another thirty guest appearances in Berlin. That will finish those damned Prussians!"

Gloria Caruso

Rupert Allan

Raoul Gunsbourg, courtly impresario, Caruso, and Camille Blanc, the first president of the Société des Bains de Mer et du Cercle des Etrangers à Monaco, who founded the opera at Monte Carlo.

Ein französischer Anschlag. (Die Schlacht am Opernhaus.) „Also abgemacht, cher Caruso, Sie geben dieses Jahr noch dreissig Gastspiele in Berlin, dann sind die verfluchten Prussiens aufgerieben!"

W. J. Henderson, critic of the *Sun*, found plenty to object to in Caruso's costumes, particularly in *La Gioconda* (left). However, when Caruso stood in the prow of his ship and saluted heaven and sea, Henderson wrote, "One cared not a whit what he wore. His delivery of that aria was the high water mark of his vocal art. It was one of the supreme pieces of singing of our time."

Opposite: Caruso as Riccardo, Count of Warwick and Governor of Boston. By some of the most ludicrous censorship interference on record, *A Masked Ball* was snatched from the Sweden of Gustav III and set in Colonial Boston. There had been an attempt on the life of Napoleon III. Would not regicide on the stage, the censor reasoned, be a deliberate incitement to real-life conspirators in the audience?

Metropolitan Opera Guild

New York Daily News

Les Huguenots is a sprawling five-hour affair with swords rattling constantly and a massacre on stage to keep the subscribers on the edge of their seats. Meyerbeer had learned early that passion combined with Papist plots made for good box-office. Like *A Masked Ball*, *Les Huguenots* requires a big cast of superlative singers. No others need apply. Caruso first sang Raoul (right) at the Metropolitan in 1905 and again in 1913.

63

The disappearance of *Martha* from the repertoire has deprived latter-day opera goers of some mighty lovely music. Caruso's singing of the romanza from the *Good Night Quartet* even on records is unforgettable. "I sung that song with all my soul," he wrote from Mexico, "and everybody were emotionated." Until Caruso, *Martha* belonged to the soprano. Patti sang it at the Metropolitan in 1892. Here, in the quartet from the 1916 revival are, left to right, Margarete Ober. Giuseppe De Luca, Caruso, and Hempel.

Culver Service

There are certain stories on which city editors in every generation will bite. A classic example is the Carmen manhandled too realistically by her Don José. Jeritza, Swarthout, and Risë Stevens have all had their innings on the front pages. With Caruso and Farrar (below) it was the other way around. After doing *Carmen* in Hollywood, Miss Farrar introduced some new stage business to her characterization, including a resounding whack on the tenor's left jaw. "Please remember, madame," the United Press reported Caruso as having said after the curtain fell, "you are not in the movies but in the Metropolitan Opera House." "If you don't like my Carmen you can get somebody else to play it," Miss Farrar flashed back. "We wouldn't think of doing that," replied the ever-courteous Caruso. "We can prevent a repetition of such scenes by getting another Don José." Of course everything was patched up.

Hamburg Opera

The Metropolitan Opera Company opened in San Francisco on April 16, 1906, with a lukewarm *Queen of Sheba.* The second night was something else again—Caruso (left) and Fremstad in *Carmen.* At 5:12 the next morning, April 18—earthquake and fire. Miraculously the company was spared, but all the scenery, properties, costumes and musical instruments were lost. The Metropolitan not only refunded on every ticket but back in New York staged a mammoth benefit for victims of the disaster. Long before Irving Berlin said so, it was a truth "There's no people like show people."

"Give me Vesuvius," Caruso shouted when he reached New York six days later and thereafter refused to sing in San Francisco ever again. The Metropolitan did not return to the West Coast for forty-two years.

Caruso was sleeping soundly when his bed began to shake. Almost petrified with fright, he finally managed to dress and make his way to Union Square. He had a towel around his neck and was clutching a signed photograph of President Theodore Roosevelt. He was better dressed in his own sketch of the disaster, above.

Arnold Genthe

The locale at left has been variously identified as Berlin and Vienna, the lady sometimes as Ada Giachetti. The American clippings do not name her. Whoever she is, wherever they are, it is an excellent shot of Caruso in motion.

Selma Kurz (shown below with Caruso) was the most celebrated lyric-coloratura soprano of Middle Europe. Unfortunately, she did not come to America until she was well past her prime and ill at that; but her success in London was as great as on her home ground.

Culver Service

New York Public Library

Lacy L. Herrmann

A Viennese program of *Masked Ball,* an opera which showed off the unending Kurz trill. She used to perambulate around the stage of Covent Garden holding it until the whole house seemed to vibrate. The last time Caruso appeared in Vienna he let it be known rather pointedly he would just as soon not sing with Frau Kurz.

Vienna's pride, the Staatsoper, bombed during World War II, rebuilt exactly as it was before and reopened in November 1955. Below: Caruso as Vasco da Gama in *L'Africana;* right: as Manrico in *Il Trovatore.* Caruso's headgear was a target for W. J. Henderson's particular wrath. The *Trovatore* picture gives some indication why.

71

His Majesty Edward VII and Queen Alexandra, before whom Caruso and Melba sang at Buckingham Palace on June 8, 1907. At left is the program. Two years before to the day Caruso had sung the third act of *La Bohème* and Act IV of *Les Huguenots* at a command performance in the palace honoring the King and Queen of Spain.

London idolized Caruso. Sir Osbert Sitwell in the third volume of his autobiography writes, ". . . Caruso and Melba, when, fat as two elderly thrushes, they trilled at each other over the hedges of tiaras, summed up in themselves the age, no less than Sargent netted it for others." But, waxing poetic, he says Caruso's voice carried in it "the warm breath of southern evenings in an orange grove, and of roses, caught in the hush of dusk at the water's edge."

BUCKINGHAM PALACE.

JUNE the 8th, 1907.

———

PROGRAMME.

———

1.	AIR	... ... (l'Africaine) ...	...	*Meyerbeer*

SIGNOR CARUSO.

2.	{ (a) "Si mes vers avaient des ailes" ...	*R. Hahn*
	{ (b) "Preghiera" (Tosca)	*Puccini*

MADAME MELBA.

3.	{ (a) "Plaisir d'Amour"	*Martini*
	{ (b) "Margoton"	*Wekerlin*

MONSIEUR GILIBERT.

4.	DUETT ... ... (La Bohème) ...	*Puccini*

MADAME MELBA and SIGNOR CARUSO.

———

At the Piano—SIGNOR BARALDI.

———

Under the Direction of MR. PAOLO TOSTI.

Royal Opera House, Covent Garden.

Nellie Melba.

Royal Opera Covent Garden

THE GRAND OPERA SYNDICATE, LIMITED.

Manager ... ... M. ANDRE MESSAGER

Secretary and Business Manager, Mr. NEIL FORSYTH

THIS EVENING'S PERFORMANCE.

Tuesday, June 7th, at 8.30

VERDI'S Opera,

RIGOLETTO

(IN ITALIAN)

Gilda	... ...	Mlle. SELMA KURZ
Giovanna	... ...	Mlle. BAUERMEISTER
Contessa di Ceprano		Mlle. HELIAN
Maddalena	...	Mme. KIRKBY LUNN
Il Duca	...	Signor CARUSO
Un Paggio	..	Miss BLISS
Sparafucile	...	M. JOURNET
Marullo	...	M. COTREUIL
Monterone	...	M. GILIBERT
Borsa	...	Signor MASIERO
Conte di Ceprano		M. DUFRICHE
Rigoletto	...	M. RENAUD
Conductor	...	Signor MANCINELLI

Stage Manager ... ... M. Almanz.

When Gatti-Casazza took over as general manager at the Metropolitan in 1908 he brought with him as first conductor Arturo Toscanini (caricatured by Caruso at right). The two were reunited with Caruso for the first time since the Scala days when Toscanini exclaimed, "By God! If that Neapolitan continues to sing like this he will make the whole world talk about him!" There was an historic production of *Cavalleria Rusticana* (opposite) during Mr. Gatti's first season. A rehearsal is shown above—reading left to right from Caruso, who holds the big bouquet of roses, are Toscanini, Emmy Destinn, Mr. Gatti, and Louise Homer. Contrast the impassioned duet with Destinn (left) with the early one on page 22.

Marziale Sisca

75

Author's Collection

Rigoletto again, with Melba and Renaud, was the vehicle for Caruso's first appearance at the Paris Opera (above) in 1908. The performance was a benefit for the Society of Authors and Composers. During the Metropolitan's 1910 Paris season he and a group of notable colleagues appeared in a big benefit (program at left) for survivors of the victims of the lost French destroyer *Pluviôse.*

Gluck's *Armide* was first produced in 1777 in Paris but had to wait for a New York production until 1910, when it opened the season at the Metropolitan. The brilliance of the cast on that occasion made it worth the wait. The principals (opposite) were Pasquale Amato, Olive Fremstad, and Enrico Caruso. Toscanini conducted. Fremstad, who created *Salome* at the Metropolitan, inspired Willa Cather's *The Song of the Lark.*

Maynard Mor

Marziale Sisca

Left: Gatti-Casazza, Belasco, Toscanini, and Puccini, the high-powered
quartet of *The Girl of the Golden
West.*

The Girl of the Golden West, based
on the play by David Belasco, had its
first performance on any stage at the
Metropolitan December 10, 1910.
Puccini himself came over to super-
vise rehearsals and the wizard of the
white forelock and clerical collar
tended to the staging. The opera house
"itself provided the finest talent in its
service to interpret the work"—Caruso, Destinn, Amato, Toscanini. The
scalpers had a field day, tickets bring-
ing up to thirty times the boxoffice
price. The record? *Girl* has been done
at the Metropolitan only thirty-four
times in seven scattered seasons.

Opposite: Caruso first undertook the lead in Massenet's *Manon* in South America in 1900. His first appearance in the part at the Metropolitan was in 1913, with Miss Farrar opposite him and Toscanini conducting. He had first sung Des Grieux in Puccini's *Manon Lescaut* in Egypt in 1895.

Farrar (above and at right) and Caruso were the strongest box-office combine in operatic history. Individually, in other company they were no drugs on the market; together they generated an excitement never equaled before or since, and when Scotti was the baritone you really had a team. *Manon* was one of their happiest collaborations.

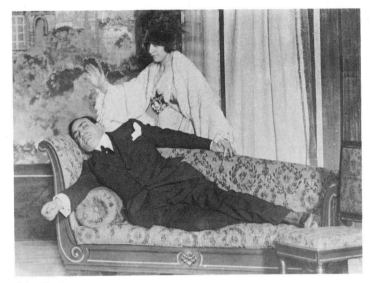

Mr. Gatti's answer to Mary Garden's success in *Louise* was a sequel to that work called *Julien.* Miss Farrar dismisses it as "a wild and confusing hodge-podge." So did the public. It went to the warehouse after five performances. Somewhere between rehearsal (left) and performance (below) the positions of the protagonists got reversed.

The first time he went to dinner at the home of his future wife, Caruso wore his *Julien* costume—"a suit of powder blue with velvet lapels," Mrs. Caruso recalls it, "with a great cloak flung across one shoulder and an enormous blue felt hat." "I wore it," Caruso confided later, "so you would remember me."

This Theatre, when filled to its capacity, can be emptied in five minutes. Choose the nearest exit now and in case of need walk quietly (do not run) to that exit in order to avoid panic.

METROPOLITAN OPERA HOVSE

GRAND OPERA SEASON 1918~1919
GIULIO GATTI-CASAZZA, General Manager

MONDAY EVENING, NOVEMBER 11TH, AT 8 O'CLOCK

SAMSON ET DALILA

OPERA IN THREE ACTS AND FOUR TABLEAUX
(IN FRENCH)

BOOK BY FERDINAND LEMAIRE

MUSIC BY C. SAINT-SAËNS

DALILA	LOUISE HOMER
SAMSON	ENRICO CARUSO
THE HIGH PRIEST	ROBERT COUZINOU (DEBUT)
ABIMELECH	ALBERT REISS
AN OLD HEBREW	LEON ROTHIER
A PHILISTINE MESSENGER	PAOLO ANANIAN
FIRST PHILISTINE	PIETRO AUDISIO
SECOND PHILISTINE	VINCENZO RESCHIGLIAN
CONDUCTOR	PIERRE MONTEUX

STAGE DIRECTOR	RICHARD ORDYNSKI
CHORUS MASTER	GIULIO SETTI
TECHNICAL DIRECTOR	EDWARD SIEDLE
STAGE MANAGER	ARMANDO AGNINI
PREMIÈRE DANSEUSE	ROSINA GALLI

PROGRAMME CONTINUED ON NEXT PAGE

CORRECT LIBRETTOS FOR SALE IN THE LOBBY
HARDMAN PIANOS USED EXCLUSIVELY

Author's Collection

Note the date on the program. It was also the opening night of the season. After the first act of *Samson and Delilah* the lights were kept lowered as a sign to the audience that some extra-curricular excitement was in the offing. The curtain rose on the full company still in their Biblical garments but carrying the flags of the Allies. The orchestra played and the company sang *The Star - Spangled Banner*, the *Marseillaise*, the *Garibaldi Hymn* and *God Save the King*. The conductor was the same Pierre Monteux who returned to the Metropolitan thirty-four years later at the age of seventy-eight.

Metropolitan Opera

On the opposite page is the maître, a young man of eighty, rehearsing *The Tales of Hoffmann* with which he opened the 1955-56 season at the Metropolitan. In the same picture, reflected in the mirror, left to right, are Osie Hawkins, Risë Stevens, Martial Singher, Cyril Ritchard, who staged the revival, Clifford Harvuot, standing, and Richard Tucker. The assistant conductor seated by Maestro Monteux is Victor Trucco.

Samson and Delilah started Caruso toward the final phase of his career.. In it he emerged a figure of larger mold than heretofore revealed. "The very shape of his head changed," says Bruno Zirato. Off stage he was still the jovial prankster but "the serious side of the man was having its way." The temptress above is Margaret Matzenauer; the Old Hebrew is Leon Rothier. At left, the blinded Samson sings, *Vois ma misère, hélas!*

Caruso had every opening night at the Metropolitan from his first season in 1903 until his last except one. He deferred in 1906 to an American girl who was making her Metropolitan debut. Miss Farrar was coming home after five years of triumphs in Germany. In his eighteen years at the Metropolitan the search for new operas for Caruso produced some strange results, as with *The Pearl Fishers* which opened the 1916-17 season, strange because in spite of Caruso's enormous popularity and beautiful singing of Bizet's music it managed to achieve only three performances. It has been on the shelf ever since. Before that, only the first two acts had been heard at the Metropolitan. Calvé sang them in 1896. The rest of the bill on that occasion was a piece of tripe called *La Navarraise* which Massenet had dished up specially for her.

The failure of *The Pearl Fishers* was no fault of the Metropolitan. Set in Ceylon, the work had been handsomely mounted and prepared. It was beautifully conducted by Giorgio Polacco, who had also been on the podium the opening night of the season before, Caruso's first Samson. As Nadir, Caruso sang "with a lyric beauty recalling his early days." *Je crois entendre encore* is still one of his most popular records. The Brahman priestess, Leila, is Frieda Hempel, and Zurga (left) Giuseppe De Luca. Unfortunately Caruso did not record the duet with his old friend but with Ancona, the baritone of the Calvé performance of 1896. De Luca, however, did make the record some ten years later with Gigli. The language of both records is Italian rather than the original French. Both are lovely. "From the depths of the temple," the duet begins.

etropolitan Opera

Alexander Eddy

O seiken iu sii bai dhi dons erli lait
huat so praudli ui heild
at dhi twailaits last glimmin
husis brod straips and
brait stars thru dhi perilos
fait—Or dhi ramparts ui
uact uere so gallontli
strimmin

And dhi Rokets red gler dhi
bombs burstin in er
ghev pruf thru dhi nait
that aur fleg was stil
dher—o se doss dhet star
spengled banner iet
ueuf or dhi lend of dhi
fri and dhi hom of dhi breuf

The lines on the opposite page are not the phonetic rendition of some Samoan war chant but our national anthem in Caruso's own delightful brand of English. This is the text he carefully drew up from many listenings and used at celebrations like the Police Games at Sheepshead Bay, August 1918 (right) or the first anniversary of Fiume Day, September 1920, at Lewisohn Stadium (opposite). Capt. Ugo D'Annunzio, the son of the poet-soldier who defended Fiume, marches at Caruso's right.

Gloria Caruso

Over There, by his friend George M. Cohan, was a Caruso favorite. On the evening of September 12, 1918, he sang it at Mayor Hylan's People's Concerts before "the largest audience ever gathered in Central Park." The same month his record of the song was released. One copy at the Waldorf auction for the *New York Sun*'s Tobacco Fund for Soldiers brought $125,000.

A sailor named Philip Gordon accompanied Caruso at a Navy Relief Society benefit in the New York Hippodrome November 3, 1918. Here they are rehearsing in Caruso's suite at the Knickerbocker Hotel. The score to the left on the piano is *La Forza del Destino* which Caruso was studying for its first performance at the Metropolitan. In spite of his generous appearances at countless benefits Caruso was still a touch "for every fund in sight." "I am not a Rockefeller," he moaned, "yet yesterday I paid $4,000 for a box of oranges for a patriotic purpose. I am worked to death."

Patriotic and Allied Benefit Performance

Metropolitan Opera House

ORGANIZED BY M. GUSTAVE HESLOUIN

TUESDAY, APRIL 17TH
1917

Programme

PREMIERE PARTIE

1. Ouverture de Phèdre . . . . . *Jules Massenet*
   Exécutée par l'Orchestre sous la direction de
   Mr. Oscar Spiresco

2. Air de Madame Butterfly . . . . *Puccini*
   chanté par Mlle. Sybil Vane

3. Variations pour violoncelle, avec accompagnement
   d'orchestra . . . . . . *Boëlman*
   exécutées par M. Maurice Dambois

4. Chant of the Deity
   Roshanara and Eva Gauthier

5. ## Mme. FRANCES ALDA
   Romances
   Au piano: M. Frank La Forge

6. Le Petit Abbè, piéce en un acte
   Stanislas . Mlle. Yvonne Garrick
   (La scène se passe dans le salon de Mlle. Guimard,
   danseuse de l'Opéra—costumes du
   XVIIIe Siècle)

7. ## M. CARUSO
   Romances
   Au piano: M. Richard Barthelemy

8. ## Mme. SARAH BERNHARDT

9. Allocution par M. Emile Villemin

10. ### POUR LE DROIT ET LA LIBERTÉ
    Grande scène patriotique
    L'Amérique: Mme. Frances Alda
    La France: Mme. Polya Frijsh
    La Belgique: Mlle. Alice Verlet
    Choeur de 500 Dames, sous la Direction de
    Mme. Clara Novello Davies

ENTR'ACTE

Frances Alda.

April 17, 1917, eleven days after the United States' entry into the first World War, there was a great benefit at the Metropolitan featuring Caruso, Alda, and Bernhardt. The cover and the first page of the program are reproduced on these pages. As the wife of the general manager of the Metropolitan, Frances Alda threw her weight around, which was considerable, and titled her autobiography *Men, Women, and Tenors*. Caruso, however, escaped her thunderbolts. Sarah Bernhardt had thumbed her nose at the German submarines to come to America for a final farewell tour. With one leg gone and the foot of the other already in the grave, she was a symbol of France's heroic resistance. Invited to Germany by the Kaiser early in her career, she replied, "When you give back Alsace and Lorraine."

Sarah Bernhardt.

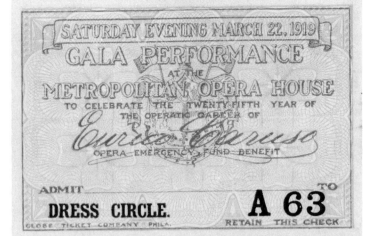

A ticket stub and the program cover (below) of Caruso's silver jubilee.

Caruso as John of Leyden.

Opposite: With Claudia Muzio in *Le Prophète*. On March 22, 1919, the Metropolitan gave Caruso a gala marking the twenty-fifth year of his career. The bill was the third act of *L'Elisir*, Act I of *Pagliacci* and the Coronation Scene from *Le Prophète*. Unbeknownst to Caruso, the evening took a peculiar turn. Mayor Hylan sent word backstage that if James M. Beck, a political enemy, appeared he would leave the opera house and the flag of the City of New York would not be presented. Mr. Beck withdrew. Caruso got the flag, his weight in silver, a kiss on the cheek from Miss Farrar, and a warm-hearted testimonial speech from Mr. Kahn in which the chairman of the board of the Metropolitan declared, "we admire the voice, the art and the man."

Joseph S. Ietti

METROPOLITAN OPERA COMPANY

Giuli Gatti-Casazza
General Manager

SPECIAL GALA PERFORMANCE
*Celebrating the Twenty-fifth Year
In the Career of*

ENRICO CARUSO

METROPOLITAN OPERA HOUSE
*Saturday Evening March the 22nd
1919*

FOR THE BENEFIT OF THE
METROPOLITAN OPERA CO.
EMERGENCY FUND

*All the contents of this programme are
copyrighted by The Theatre Magazine Co.*

Marziale Sisca

Rodrigo de Llano

94

Mexico's biggest theater was in danger of bursting at the seams, so the enterprising impresario moved Caruso to the bull ring where 22,000 people at a time thronged to hear him. At his final performance November 2, 1919, 25,000 somehow got in. "What explosion!" Caruso wrote home of his Mexican debut. "Everybody was creazy and we stop to sing for a while. I got my public from this moment. At the end of the act which I put two top notes very strong and beautifully the entusiasm was to the zenit. But my heart! He jomping terribly and nearly I felt down. . . ." The panorama above was made by splicing two frames of a home-made movie. At left is the improvised stage; at right, Caruso and the Roman contralto, Gabriella Besanzoni, in *Samson and Delilah*.

Rosa Ponselle

La Forza del Destino did not make its entry at the Metropolitan until Mr. Gatti produced it for Caruso, November 15, 1918. The importance of the evening, however, lay in the debut of an American girl who until her audition had never set foot inside the Metropolitan but twice in her life. For nearly twenty years she stayed on as the top dramatic soprano. Her name is Rosa Ponselle. Above, the finale of *Forza,* Ponselle, Caruso, and Mardones.

Metropolitan Opera House

SPECIAL PERFORMANCE
IN HONOR OF
HIS ROYAL HIGHNESS THE PRINCE OF WALES

Tuesday Evening, November 18th at 9 o'clock

PROGRAMME

1. OBERON ....*Weber*
   OVERTURE
   Scene 3, Act 1: Hall in the Harem of the Caliph
   REZIA ....FLORENCE EASTON
   FATIMA ....KATHLEEN HOWARD
   Conductor—ARTUR BODANZKY

2. SAMSON ET DALILA ....*Saint-Saens*
   Ballet and Chorus from Scene 2, Act 3: Interior of Temple of Dagon
   Incidental Dance by LILYAN OGDEN, and the Corps de Ballet
   Conductor—GIUSEPPE BAMBOSCHEK

3. PAGLIACCI ....*Leoncavallo*
   Act 1. Outskirts of a Village in Calabria
   NEDDA ....FLORENCE EASTON
   CANIO ....ENRICO CARUSO
   TONIO ....PASQUALE AMATO
   BEPPE ....GIORDANO PALTRINIERI
   SILVIO ....MARIO LAURENTI
   Conductor—ROBERTO MORANZONI

PROGRAMME CONTINUED ON NEXT PAGE   HARDMAN PIANO USED EXCLUSIVELY

Author's Collection

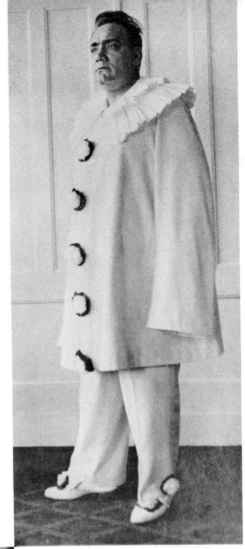

Wide World Photos

European Picture Service

The Prince of Wales (left), later Edward VIII, now Duke of Windsor, on his first visit to New York in 1919, during which the Metropolitan gave a special performance in his honor (see program above). Although he had opened the season in *Tosca* the night before, Caruso obliged with the first act of *Pagliacci,* bowed low on his curtain call in the direction of the royal box with his hands folded on his chest.

97

Will these great artists
sing in your home
on Christmas morning?

Victrola XVII, $275
Victrola XVII, electric, $332.50
Mahogany or oak

Will Caruso thrill you? Alma Gluck or John McCormack play upon your heart strings? Harry Lauder regale you with his inimitable fun? Victor Herbert's Orchestra invite you to the lovely cadences of immortal melodies? Sousa stir your good American blood with "The Stars and Stripes Forever"?

The opera, the symphony orchestra, the violin, the piano, the military band, the dance orchestra, the vaudeville stage—the Victrola brings you the shining lights of them all! The foremost artists of the world make Victrola Records exclusively.

Your Christmas will be merrier for the Victrola. And it will be but the beginning of a long and happy companionship between your household and all the master-magicians of music and entertainment.

Victors and Victrolas
$12 to $950

Victor dealers
everywhere

Victor Talking Machine Company
Camden, N. J., U. S. A.

Victor
"HIS MASTER'S VOICE"
REG. U.S. PAT. OFF.

Victrola

RCA Victor

In less than a score of years Caruso established the financial security of the Victor company and the Metropolitan. He gave respectability to recording. Before his time the artists were a little sheepish about singing into the horn (right), somewhat as the "legitimate" actors were at baring their emotions before the primitive movie cameras. Above, a stellar cast assembles in Camden, January 25, 1917, to record the Sextet from *Lucia* and the *Rigoletto* Quartet. Left to right: De Luca, Galli-Curci, Caruso, Flora Perini, Angelo Bada, and Minnie Egener. Journet, the bass, is absent.

99

100

Not even Jesse Lasky (below) could make a movie star out of Caruso, although it must be said his acting was far ahead of the rest of the cast or the script. In *My Cousin* he played a dual role, a famous tenor and his impoverished sculptor cousin. It opened with great fanfare at the Rivoli in New York and was plugged mercilessly in the trade press and elsewhere. "Few films," says the Museum of Modern Art Film Library, "ever enjoyed less success." His second picture, a little number entitled *A Splendid Romance*, was never released.

Irving Kolodin

Peabody Institute Library

CARUSO IN TOWN TODAY

First Appearance in N. E. Pennsylvania

Tonight at Armory, 8:15

CARUSO

(Himself)

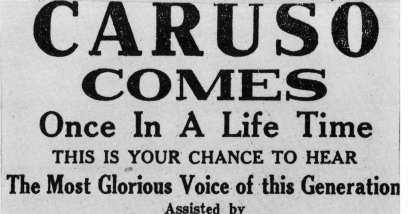

CARUSO COMES
Once In A Life Time
THIS IS YOUR CHANCE TO HEAR
The Most Glorious Voice of this Generation
Assisted by
MADAME BIANCHINI-CAPPELLI, Dramatic Soprano, and MISS RUTH DEYO, the Brilliant Young American Pianist.

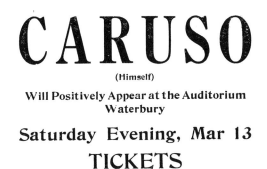

CARUSO
(Himself)
Will Positively Appear at the Auditorium Waterbury

Saturday Evening, Mar 13
TICKETS
at STEINERT'S, 55 West Main St, Phone 3079.   Evenings after 6 o'clock at Prentzel's residence, 48 Park Place, Phone 3026.

Special Trains from Surrounding Towns

$2,000 Have been deposited with the Waterbury National Bank as a guarantee that Caruso will appear as advertised above.

A Caruso concert was no intellectual exercise. Invariably he shared the platform with a violinist and a soprano, usually Nina Morgana, now Mrs. Bruno Zirato. The pattern was rigid. The violinist would render a selection, the soprano a number, Caruso an aria. This order was repeated. Then intermission. The second half was the same as the first except cut in half—violinist, soprano, Caruso, one time around. If Caruso felt like it, and there was time, he would add a few Neapolitan songs as encores and catch the train to the next town. The fee? $7,000. Opposite, the crowd in Fort Worth's cow palace, 8,000 persons. Right, arriving in St. Paul, May 8, 1919, with Miss Morgana for a concert. One of his assisting artists was a young violinist named Francis Cugat. He is now occupied with another kind of music and is known as Xavier Cugat.

Bruno Zirato

No one, least of all Caruso,
suspected this Christmas Eve
performance of *La Juive*
would be his last.

METROPOLITAN OPERA HOUSE

GRAND OPERA SEASON 1920~1921
GIULIO GATTI-CASAZZA General Manager

FRIDAY EVENING, DECEMBER 24TH AT 8 O'CLOCK

LA JUIVE
(THE JEWESS)

OPERA IN FOUR ACTS AND FIVE SCENES BY EUGENE SCRIBE
(IN FRENCH)

MUSIC BY JACQUES F. HALEVY

RACHEL	FLORENCE EASTON
ELEAZAR	ENRICO CARUSO
CARDINAL BROGNI	LEON ROTHIER
THE PRINCESS	EVELYN SCOTNEY
LEOPOLD	ORVILLE HARROLD
RUGGIERO	ROBERT LEONHARDT
ALBERT	MILLO PICCO
A HERALD	PAOLO ANANIAN
MAJOR DOMO	

EMPEROR SIGISMUND, CITIZENS OF CONSTANCE, JEWS AND
JEWESSES, NOBLES, PRIESTS, SOLDIERS, THE EXECUTIONER

CONDUCTOR . . . . . . ARTUR BODANZKY

STAGE DIRECTOR	SAMUEL THEWMAN
CHORUS MASTER	GIULIO SETTI
TECHNICAL DIRECTOR	EDWARD SIEDLE
STAGE MANAGER	ARMANDO AGNINI
PREMIERE DANSEUSE	ROSINA GALLI
PREMIER DANSEUR	GIUSEPPE BONFIGLIO

PROGRAMME CONTINUED ON NEXT PAGE

CORRECT LIBRETTOS FOR SALE IN THE LOBBY

HARDMAN PIANOS USED EXCLUSIVELY

Author's Collection

Metropolitan Opera

The last opera he studied and the last he ever sang was *La Juive*. To make the Passover scene (above) as authentic as possible he went straight to the orthodox synagogues. Every gesture, every detail of his costume was perfect. Eléazar was one of his towering achievements. According to Mrs. Caruso, *Rachel, quand du Seigneur* was his favorite of the arias he recorded. The soprano in his last performance was not Ponselle (opposite), who sang the first *Juive* with him, but Florence Easton. Only the year before Easton had been Nedda to his Canio in the gala for the Prince of Wales.

105

At the age of nine Sarah Bernhardt adopted as a motto *Quand même*—
"even so." It was emblazoned on the curtain of her theater and on the can-
opy above her bed, perhaps the best device with which an artist ever armed
himself to face the world. What it said in words this Caruso photograph
comes close to expressing. It seems to sum up the mystic relationship between artist and public, that curious blend of humility and pride, of mis-
trust and belief—"even so."

CHAPTER III

OFF STAGE

No ARTIST WITHIN MEMORY EVER KINDLED THE RAPPORT WITH HIS PUBLIC THAT CARUSO did. No barrier of footlights or anything else stood between them. One Saturday night after an *Aida* the curtain calls were stretching out longer than usual. After about the dozenth Caruso good-naturedly rubbed his stomach as if to say, "I'm hungry now. Please go home and let me have my supper." The fans roared their approval and the house lights went up.

These informal communications were by no means confined to pantomime on his part. More than once in the third act of *L'Elisir d'Amore* when the audience demanded a repeat of "Una furtiva lagrima" he would confide, "I can't; they won't let me." This was after Toscanini had done his work and forever banished encores at the Metropolitan as he had in Milan.

Nor was the direction all one-way. On the evening of December 19, 1919, Caruso was again singing *L'Elisir*. He had given a brilliant performance, exceptional even by his standards, and for a very good reason. For the same reason the ovation was tremendous. There was not a soul in the big auditorium who did not know his news that evening and rejoice with him. Gloria had made her appearance the night before. *"Viva pappa!"* the shouts rolled down galleries and loges alike.

No event in his life was allowed to go uncommented upon. While he was singing in Cuba the summer of 1920 his house in Easthampton was robbed of jewelry estimated in value by the newspapers at the time between $236,000 and $500,000. No official statement was ever made as to the exact loss, and although the papers never said it in so many words the notion was widespread that it might have been an inside job. Caruso's only concern was the safety of his wife and baby. "Lots of jewels will come," he cabled.

His first date after he got back to New York was a recital at Ocean Grove. Those ancient timbers reverberated more to Methodist hymns than to any other harmonies, but the sprawling old tabernacle on the Jersey shore was always hospitable to the greats of opera and concert, the camp-meeting schedule permitting.

That August night Caruso was singing, as he often did in recital, Rodolfo's "Narrative" from *La Bohème.* There is a phrase as he approaches the climax in which the poet tells Mimi, ". . . your lovely eyes have robbed me of all my jewels." When Caruso came to that line he could not resist. Neither could the audience. Almost imperceptibly he shrugged his shoulders, assumed a rueful expression and ever so slightly turned his open palms to the public. The roof came down.

Caruso's only pupil was Ed McNamara, the singing cop from Paterson, New Jersey. While he was still in uniform McNamara used to electioneer in saloons for Senator William Hughes. On the nights he wasn't so engaged he would go to the non-Hughes taverns and heckle the opposition. It was probably senatorial influence or perhaps the equally weighty intercession of Madame Schumann-Heink, who discovered McNamara at a sort of Jersey May festival, that got him a hearing. Pressure or no pressure, you may be sure Caruso would never have accepted him had he not thought the strapping young hopeful had a good voice, which McNamara did—and big.

Mac finally gave up music—or, more accurately, music gave him up. Thereafter he became a highly succcessful actor playing, of all things, cops. On stage, as in real life, he never made an arrest. It was type-casting. His sergeant in Paterson once complained that the only time McNamara's name ever appeared on the station-house blotter was payday. No one who saw it will ever forget that first act speakeasy in *Strictly Dishonorable*. "I thought," a bibulous judge rebuked him, "policemen never drank."

"It just seems like never," was Mac's sharp reply.

In the so-called "musical subjects" Mac was a bigger dud than most singers, which is saying something. Once in a sight-reading lesson with Buzzi-Peccia (Deems Taylor is authority for this one) the maestro stopped him.

"Mr. McNamara," he warned, "that is a dotted eighth. You will please to treat it as such."

"That," Mac blurted, "is one man's opinion!"

Some idea of the size of his voice may be gathered from the fact that Caruso constantly insisted his pupil sing with less force. *"Piano, piano,"* he would plead, "not so loud." Remembering the block-busters Caruso used to release even on records, one wonders just what the McNamara instrument was like that his mentor should want it soft-pedaled.

One day Caruso reversed himself. "Louder, louder!" he kept urging. When the chandeliers were coming loose and the windows beginning to rattle, Mac, somewhat mystified, asked, "Why, Mr. Caruso? I thought you told me to hold back."

"I know," Caruso gleefully replied, "but Scotti's home today," pointing to the apartment below, "and he's sick."

Another time he counseled, "Mac, you go to the bathroom in the morning. You push down. When you come to the high note, *push up!*" This is about as close as Caruso ever got to codifying his vocal method.

"The social man in him was irresistible," Huneker said of Caruso. "His company was a tonic for all ailments," Tetrazzini testified. "A simplicity which sprang from innate kindness," is what Geraldine Farrar remembers.

The stories of his generosity are legion. His bounty was like Antony's. There was no winter in it. An autumn indeed it was, that grew the more by reaping.

"Even in his caricatures he shows the sweetness of his nature," Victor Herbert said at a dinner which the Lotos Club gave in Caruso's honor. "He has never drawn me as fat as others have."

On a June afternoon just six months before she died I heard from Mrs. Caruso herself some of the stories I had loved in her book and some that were new to me. She was staying at the Pavilion Henri IV in St. Germain-en-Laye, half an hour from Paris. Like her adored Rico she was making a brave fight for life. No one will ever know whether or not she realized how ill she was. The eyes were as blue as everybody had told me they would be, her manner as direct and winning.

Through her kindness I found Martino Ceccanti, Caruso's old valet and friend, in Florence. Together we journeyed up to the villa at Signa. We walked through the gardens which were Caruso's pride, past the courts where Princess Marie José later played tennis, the bocce court where Marshal Badoglio often relaxed. As we left, Martino, gentleman's gentleman as ever was, thanked the caretaker. "I know it would make him happy," he said, "to see it so beautifully kept."

From boyhood, Caruso was a miracle of order. Throughout his career he kept his own accounts and scrapbooks. Bruno Zirato, managing director of the New York Philharmonic-Symphony, who served as his secretary, recalls an entry in his personal ledger. "Expenses for my marriage . . . $50.00." In all his career he never asked for a complimentary ticket. Earle R. Lewis, former assistant manager of the Metropolitan, says the ticket bill for his performances ran eight to nine thousand dollars a season. He handed them out by the fistful to friends able as well as unable to pay their own way. He was the grand seigneur.

Toward the end he gave up the handsome big tooled-leather scrapbooks which were made especially for him and, instead, mounted his cuttings on big leaves of heavy gray paper. The last clipping he pasted up was from the *Brooklyn Eagle* of December 12, 1920. It told of his appearance at the Academy of Music the night before when he had begun to bleed at the mouth. The audience was dismissed after the first act but not until Caruso in full view of everyone had filled towel after towel with blood in a superhuman effort to finish the performance.

He and Mrs. Caruso drove back to their apartment in the Vanderbilt Hotel, never once mentioning the fearful events of the evening. It was a nightmare to be forgotten as quickly as possible. He ordered supper as usual. It might have been any of hundreds of nights after a performance, except that it was early and he was not smoking.

That was a Saturday. He was scheduled to sing the following Monday. He did.

Such was his sense of responsibility to the management, the public and himself. He was the most expensive artist of his time and the cheapest. His record of cancellations was almost zero. And to the end he kept his head in the face of such adulation as few champions in any field have ever known.

Caruso's picture on a sheet music cover was a sure boost to sales. Tosti, Buzzi-Peccia and the tenor himself were the chief composers to benefit from this use of his likeness and name. The last was somebody named Jack Stanley. His mawkish contribution was *They Needed a Songbird in Heaven* with the subtitle (*So God Took Caruso Away*).

Alexander Eddy

Culver Service

Although they don't particularly look it, the characters above comprise perhaps the most uneasy passenger list since the ark. The outbreak of the First World War caught practically the entire roster of the Metropolitan Opera Company scattered over the map of Europe. North Atlantic waters being far too heavily infested with submarines, Mr. Gatti frantically summoned his songbirds to Naples. Together they set sail from there on H. M. S. S. *Canopic* October 20, 1914, and landed in Boston thirteen days later. This priceless photograph was made by Giulio Setti, chorus master of the Metropolitan. Center stage, appropriately, is Mr. Gatti in the gray hat and coat. Sheltered by the general manager's ample paunch is Caruso. To Mr. Gatti's left is Toscanini and in the foreground holding the camera is Giorgio Polacco. Behind Maestro Polacco is Elisabeth Schumann. Back of her are Frieda Hempel (left), and Geraldine Farrar (right). The enchanting creature in the middle of the back row is Lucrezia Bori.

111

Neither the famous moustache nor monocle being visible, we have to take the photographer's word that the man embracing Caruso (left) is Andres de Segurola. After his career as a singer de Segurola went out to Hollywood where he opened a vocal studio and acted in a few movies. While playing Grace Moore's pragmatic maestro in *One Night of Love,* his best-known pupil in real life was Deanna Durbin. Caruso did not always arrive smiling, as witness the shot below on a German ship.

Above, taking the air in Berlin. Caruso's German manager, Emil Ledner, is at left. The more Germanic type at right is unidentified in Caruso's snapshot album. Ledner published a book of recollections of Caruso the year after the tenor died, in which he modestly claimed Caruso's world fame began with his German appearances. In addition to Berlin, Caruso sang in Dresden, Leipzig, Hamburg, Frankfurt-am-Main, Nuremberg, Munich, and Stuttgart. His career in Germany was halted only by the First World War, his last appearances there having been in the autumn of 1913. At right, one of the earliest of the clowning pictures with which he obliged photographers and public even under the shadow of death. A poor photograph of Caruso is as hard to come by as an inferior recording of his voice. He gave to the camera.

113

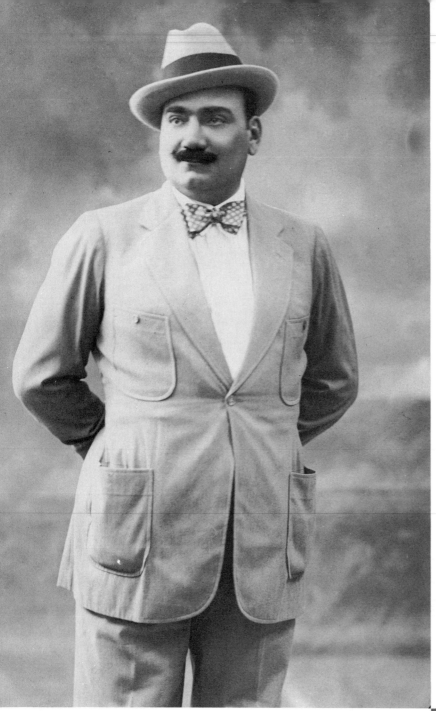

Marziale Sisca

"Never shall I forget the apparition that walked into the first rehearsal," Geraldine Farrar says of the Caruso circa 1904. Shrieking checks, a gray fedora, and yellow gloves clasping a gold-headed cane are among the details Miss Farrar noted. A passport photographer would be ashamed of the effort at right.

114

There is a bit of Al Capone in the outfit below. In point of time this may have been after Scotti got him to his London tailor, but it hasn't begun to show. Things got better, but the noisy dresser in him would occasionally break out.

Marziale Sisca

Marziale Sisca

His hats could be as strange as his stage headgear.

The source of this picture captioned it as Enrico, Jr., at the age of four, with his father and mother in London. Some years later in a magazine article the lady was identified as Miss Louise Saer, the children's governess. She is actually Mrs. Albert J. Weber. The Weber family were close friends of Caruso.

This unusual informal shot is by a Paris photographer, the year and circumstances unknown, but it captures Caruso in a wonderfully characteristic expression, quizzical and even a little shy. It is probably breakfast, for his left hand clutches what looks like the remains of a *croissant,* and the big cup might hold *café au lait.*

At the door of his Lancia. He was an incessant smoker—Egyptian cigarettes, two packs a day, always in a holder. He even smoked in the dressing room. Before a performance he would take an inhalant, then a pinch of Swedish snuff to clear the nostrils. A gargle of salt in lukewarm water, a sip of diluted Scotch, and he was ready for the stage.

Alexander Eddy

A studio pose, 1905. The moustache came and went almost with the seassons. The photograph is inscribed to Gustave Kobbé, critic of the *New York Herald,* whose *Opera Singers* and *Complete Opera Book* went into countless editions. The current version of the latter was revised by the Earl of Harewood.

Caruso was as susceptible to a balcony as Mussolini, fortunately for different reasons. The shot at left from his personal album was taken at Salsomaggiore in 1910. He also impersonated Nero on the same balcony. Above, a remarkable simulation of another emperor. Below, he gives his blessing to Emmy Destinn and Dinh Gilly, a big bruiser of a baritone from Algeria. It was about the only blessing this union ever got.

Definitely not the Wright Brothers; in fact, Caruso's dashing pilot is un-
named. It may have been lucky for Caruso, if not for us, that he came before
the days of rapid transit. During the Metropolitan season he did not divide
his time between continents as many of the artists do today. Sooner or later,
it is bound to tell in the artistic results.

119

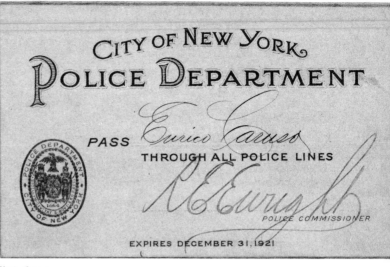

Caruso's proudest honor was a captaincy in the New York Police Department. "Can I arrest people now?" he asked Commissioner Enright as he received his badge. When told he could, he gleefully announced, "Then I go to the Metropolitan right away and get Mr. Gatti."

Caruso in Saratoga, 1918.

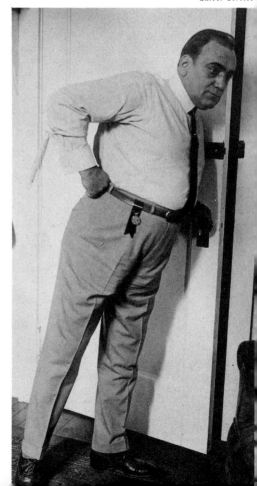

Those three-hour luncheons at Del Pezzo's are beginning to show at right. A large table was kept for him there, Thirty-fourth Street in those days, whether he showed up or not. He shunned exercise. "Friendly remonstrance was of no avail," Zirato remembers. "He would listen and occasionally nod affirmatively—and that was an end to the matter."

120

Another reward of fame (above): Caruso balked at a first-person role in the movies but allowed himself to turn up as himself in the funny papers. Race horses were named for him. Below, Giulio Setti seems to be taking his life in his hands with Caruso at the wheel. Actually Caruso never learned to drive.

The beautiful Villa Campi at Lastra a Signa near Florence, which Caruso acquired in 1904 and renamed Bellosguardo. Its gardens and goodly walks continually are green.

The Knickerbocker Hotel (below), now the Newsweek Building, was Caruso's home from 1908 until it was sold in 1920, a transaction which the tenor regarded as a personal affront. He had a fourteen-room apartment on the ninth floor and from the corner balcony sang *The Star-Spangled Banner* to the crowd in Times Square on the false Armistice in 1918.

Caruso spreads himself in the Milan sunlight, 1915. How different from the days when as a struggling young artist he was avoided in the Galleria. The big moustache at left is Enrico Scognamillo, one of his cronies.

At the famous Empire style white piano made for him by Hardman, Peck & Company.

Alexander Eddy

The world's greatest singer shows his medals.
In his time six nations bestowed eleven honors on Caruso—Italy, France, Belgium,
Spain, England, and Germany. From the
United States came only the New York police commission, but Mrs. Caruso says it
pleased him more than any other recognition.

Caruso collected everything—coins, bronzes,
jeweled watches, enameled snuffboxes, tear
bottles, old velvets and embroideries. Much
of this loot was housed in a special gallery
in Fiftieth Street near Fifth Avenue, but here
he is before a choice cabinet in his hotel
suite.

What Mardi Gras is to New Orleans the Metropolitan is to Atlanta. Caruso helped make it so. At left is Pasquale Amato and at right Leon Rothier. Opera stars today still rock themselves on the porch of the hotel appropriately named Georgian Terrace.

Caruso and Lucrezia Bori (below), at the Federal Penitentiary in Atlanta when Caruso sang for the inmates April 23, 1913. The notice of that unique concert in the prison newspaper, *Good Words,* was in verse, the poet-critic identified only as Reg. No. 4435. Several seasons later Miss Farrar sang there. The warden wrote that her *Annie Laurie* was "worth a hundred sermons."

Musical America

ystone Pictures, Inc.

With Otto H. Kahn, the Metropolitan's chairman of the board and its greatest patron.

Marziale Sisca

126

Toscanini, Caruso, and Scognamillo.

The baritone Antonio Scotti was perhaps Caruso's closest friend. A fellow Neapolitan but with a good deal more suavity, Scotti helped bring about Caruso's first Covent Garden engagement and introduced him to his London tailor, Scholte, about the time of the photograph opposite. At right, Scotti in *Manon Lescaut* as seen by the photographer, and below, as immortalized by Caruso.

This one was made by a boardwalk photographer in Atlantic City in 1910. Caruso's face was a contradiction. His complexion was lighter than that of most southern Italians. The fine line of his lips and the noble brow were more Roman than Neapolitan.

Caruso's only pupil was Ed McNamara, the singing cop from Paterson, N. J., who later became a well-known actor. Here he is with his discoverer, Madame Schumann-Heink.

Right: At Sheepshead Bay with Bruno Zirato, his secretary from 1917 until his death. He served as Caruso's best man. When Mr. Zirato was married to Nina Morgana in June of 1921 Caruso returned the compliment by being his secretary's best man *in absentia* and supplying the wedding ring. Mr. Zirato is managing director of the New York Philharmonic-Symphony.

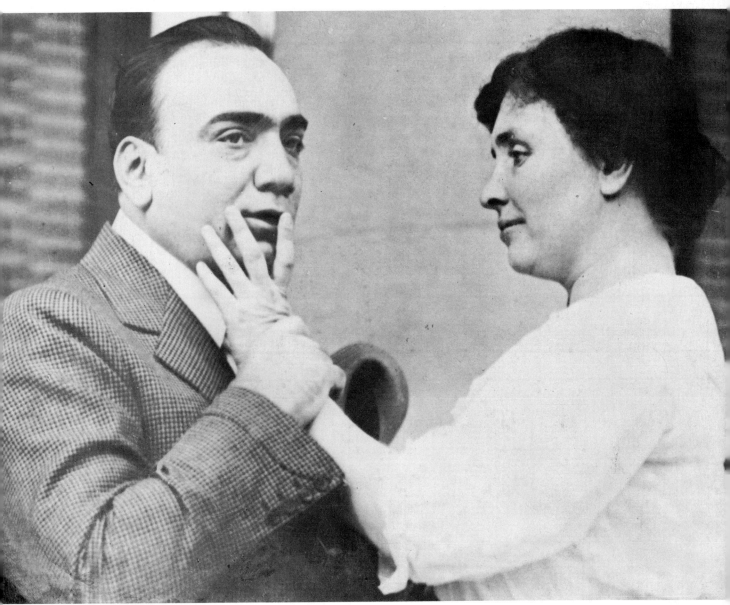

New York Herald Tribune

"What a magnificent experience it was when with ravished fingers I felt Caruso's voice in passages from *Samson!*" said Helen Keller. "Spellbound, I followed him as in a perfect glory of tone he sang compassion for the captive, lamenting his loss of vision and the strength with which he had wrought in the light of day. Then Caruso's voice swelled and surged in harmonious billows as he sang of Samson's reviving courage and the might with which in the dark he tugged the pillars of the temple until the roof crashed down on his enemies, the Philistines. Indeed it was unforgettable, the animation of Caruso's face and his rapt response to the 'sphere-born, harmonious sisters, voice and verse.' " Tears in his eyes, Caruso said afterward, "I have sung the best in my life for you."

Caruso was married to Dorothy Park Benjamin August 20, 1918, in the Marble Collegiate Church, New York. The delightful fore and aft views of the couple on their wedding day were made on the roof of the Knickerbocker Hotel. Six months later they were married according to the rites of the Roman Catholic Church in St. Patrick's Cathedral.

Their only child, Gloria Caruso, was born December 18, 1919.
Here is the family at East Hampton the following summer.

131

Martino Ceccanti

Martino Ceccanti was with Caruso from 1905 until the tenor's death. More than a valet, he became the overseer of Villa Bellosguardo. Life with Caruso took more than skill and patience; sometimes it required courage of a high order, as in the San Francisco earthquake and fire, and in 1910 when Caruso was threatened by the Black Hand. It was Martino who made the trip alone to Brooklyn to leave the bundle of fake bills in the designated spot. Above, he is shown in 1906 (left) and in 1955 (right) when the author visited him in Florence.

132   Gloria.

Caruso and his bride of less than two weeks at the Police Reserve games, Sheepshead Bay, August 31, 1918.

Gloria and her two sons, January 1957: Eric Dunmore Murray, twelve, called Ricki, and Colin Duncan Alexander Murray, eight, nicknamed Coco.

THIS CHECK IS IN PAYMENT OF ACCOUNT AS LISTED BELOW AND THE ENDORSEMENT THEREON
CONSTITUTES A RECEIPT. **PLEASE DETACH CHECK BEFORE DEPOSITING.**

*Feb 17
1915* — *Pagliacci Mat Ein Feb 17* — 2000
a/c advance — 275-
2275

Benissima

Grande ovazione

ultimo

Bruno Zirato

It was Caruso's custom to comment on each of his performances on the voucher of his check. *Pagliacci* on February 17, 1915, is rated as "best," "great ovation," and *"ultimo"* which is about as high as you can go.

---

*Samson et Dalila
Premier acte
Scène I*

Samson est parmi les Hébreux sur la place publique de la ville de Gaza en Palestine

Apres le corale des Hebreux qui finisse avec les mots " Divins serments par nos aieux recus!. et precisement sur les huit mesures de musique joué par l'orchestre, Samson sortant de la foule dis:

Arrêter | ô mes frères | Et benissele nom Du Dieu saint de nos | pères!) Car l'heure du par|don Est peut-être arri-|vée.! — | — Oui, j'ent

Gloria Caruso

This is how Caruso learned his parts. He copied everything in a notebook which went with him everywhere. On train rides, boat trips, anywhere he might find a little study period, out came the black book. Caruso was no waster of time.

---

tends dans mon coeur une | voix êli vée — | — C'est la | voix du Sei-gneur | qui parle par ma | bouche de ce Dieu plein de bon+té Que | la prière | touche> pro+met la liber-té — | Frères | brisous nos | chaines — Et+ rele+vous l'au+ tel Du seul | Dieu d'Israël — 24 — | L'as-tu | donc oublié | Celui dont la puis | sance se | fit tou all+ é | — | Lui qui | plein de clé-

Caruso was never happier than at his desk drawing or pasting up his scrap-books. He assembled several volumes of World War I cartoons. They show a mind with a sense of history. He never took money for his caricatures but gave them away prodigally, mainly to his friend Marziale Sisca for publication in *La Follia*.

Marziale Sisca

Paul Seligman

One day Caruso saw in the window of an autograph shop a caricature he had made of President Wilson. He waited outside while Mrs. Caruso went in and inquired the price. When he heard $75 he was delighted. "That is good pay for ten minutes," he beamed. "Better we stop singing and draw." He also worked in bronze (right)—and he had no illusions about himself.

135

Naples, which had given him life, received him at the end. The beauty of her matchless bay for a time bestowed new life and hope. "Come back to Sorrento . . ." Here the stricken warrior would find health again. June and most of July, 1921, at the Vittoria Hotel (above), were happy days for Caruso and his little family, but that happiness ended swiftly.

CHAPTER IV

THE LAST YEAR

O N AUGUST 3, 1920, IN A LETTER TO BRUNO ZIRATO REPRODUCED ON PAGE 141 OF THIS
book, Caruso complained of *"dolore in genere"*—"pain all over." He was not long back from
a month's engagement in Havana but there was no rest for the weary. He embarked late September
on a concert tour. There were only twelve dates, but what an itinerary—Montreal, Toronto, Chicago, St. Paul, Denver, Omaha, Tulsa, Fort Worth, Houston, two in Charlotte, and Norfolk. Before
he left he got in a recording session at Camden.

Always hypersensitive to criticism, he was upset by a trio of bad reviews when the opera
season opened. "If I sing as those critics say I do," he served notice, "it is time I appeared no more
before the New York public." Mr. Gatti was panic-stricken. Eventually Caruso was dissuaded.

There were six performances in the opera house, then the night of horror in Brooklyn.
Intercostal neuralgia, his physician diagnosed it. "Intercostal neuralgia," Mrs. Caruso repeated it
bitterly to me thirty-four years later. "It became a kind of incantation."

Christmas Eve he sang *La Juive*. Bodanzky, the conductor, visited his dressing room at
intermission. Caruso was bolt upright in a chair, weeping with pain. "If it's your throat," Bodanzky
asked, "why are you holding your side?" Too bad the doctors were not as scientific.

The celebration of Christmas went on as in years past—the gold pieces had to be put in
the little coin boxes, hundreds of them, for everybody at the Metropolitan—until shortly after
noon. A bloodcurdling scream rent the air. Let the patient himself tell the story, a letter to his
brother, published here for the first time:

THE VANDERBILT HOTEL
NEW YORK

1 February 1921
From the convalescent bed.

Dear Giovanni,

From the day of Christmas until today I have suffered nothing but torture. I will tell you what
has happened.

For some time I have not been well partly because of pains in the right flank which were bothering me a few weeks before Christmas, and partly because of the profuse bleeding in my throat. This made me worry in spite of seeing the doctor every day who told me it was nothing.

On Christmas Day, which I hoped to pass as a most beautiful feast because, besides a big Christmas tree with presents for friends and children, my wife had placed under the fireplace a Nativity with very large shepherds which I have no idea where she found. Everything pointed to a splendid Christmas. On the Eve I had sung *La Juive* and we dined afterwards, but towards 12:30 I found myself in the dining room where I was giving presents to the servants when I noted a pain I had never had . . . I arrived in my bathroom. I began to wash my mouth, but that strange illness took me again and then I decided to throw myself into hot water. I drew a tepid bath and got in, but did not have the time to sit myself down when I doubled over forward like a dry twig, screaming like a madman. Everyone from the household came running and they pulled me out. They tried to make me stand but I was bent over holding my left flank with my left hand and was letting out howls like a wounded dog, so loud they heard me on the street from the eighteenth floor and throughout the whole hotel. They made me sit on a chaise lounge where I could stay only on the edge and always bent forward.

My doctor was called by telephone, and he was not at home. The doctor of the hotel was found who, not knowing my illness and not knowing me, did not hazard to give me anything, but it seems that he gave me a palliative until my doctor arrived. If someone had not insisted upon calling another doctor I would have been nice and cold in Brooklyn.* Returning to my story, my doctor arrived and said as he had said before that it was an intercostal pain and therefore with a sedative it would pass.

Five days I was between life and death because of the stubbornness of that good doctor. Finally after the second day, my wife, with the help of my Italian friends, who took turns at being on hand, held various consultations. The last doctor said, 'If this man is not operated on in twelve hours he is gone.' Thought was then given to the surgeon. He was found. He had to have the consent of my wife to operate and when he had it he went to work. It was a case of breaking two ribs because they came to the conclusion that I had a purulent pleurisy and the fluid had begun to reach the heart. What a mess. I screamed for five days, seated at the edge of my couch day and night. Finally what I remember is this: sounds of instruments being moved and jarred, and then as if they had placed the point of the knife in the spleen, and then great shouts of 'Hurrah.' What happened was that in making the incision to get to the ribs, the pus came out like an explosion striking the doctor, everything, the whole room. There was no need to cut the ribs which would have been painful and this indicates the speed of my convalescence.

Do you know what pleurisy is? It is what we commonly call a pain in the flank. But there are various kinds. Mine was the most disgusting because for years I was carrying it around and it was the cause of all my troubles. Now I feel fairly well. I eat like a wolf in order to gain weight because I have lost many kilograms. And already I am beginning to walk about the room staying four hours a day seated in the sun, when there is any, or else in the sitting room playing with Gloria. The wound has reached its last stages but it must be open for any eventuality. It will take another month to close itself. The month of March, one half I will spend at the seashore, and one half on the boat coming over there. This is the story and I hope you are well and know that until a tooth falls out nothing serious will have happened.†

Tell Bettina that I thank her for her affectionate letter and that she should share in this letter also.

---

* Well before this time interment had been prohibited on Manhattan Island and great burying grounds had grown up in Brooklyn, Queens and Westchester.

† The allusion to a tooth is dead serious. The year before on his forty-seventh birthday Caruso gave reporters a dental exhibition. "Samson's strength was in his hair," he said. "Mine is in my teeth. I have never had a toothache in my life. My perfect teeth have contributed greatly to my good health, and my good health has sustained me in my art. I really believe that when one of these teeth I have shown you goes I go. Caruso is finished. But they are strong yet."

Kisses to the children.

I embrace you and kiss you with affection.

Your

ENRICO

I pray you to read this letter also to Maria,‡ because I cannot answer or write to all.

Caruso's brave mind and spirit were about two months ahead of his body's schedule. It had been necessary to remove a rib which he did not know about until weeks later. In all, he had undergone six operations, only three of which had been made known to the public at the time. There were circulars daily, sometimes oftener, just as for royalty. He was not able to sail for Italy until May 28. Mr. Gatti, departing earlier in the month, had issued a windy statement: "Enrico Caruso will without any doubt again take his glorious post at the Metropolitan."

Before he left, Caruso paid a visit to the opera house. Even off-season the Metropolitan is a good-sized family. From all over they came running as the news shot through the theater, "Mr. Caruso is here!" The comptroller locked the safe and closed shop. The Fortieth Street stage door was left unattended. The porters dropped their mops and brooms.

"How wonderful you look, Mr. Caruso!" was the exclamation on all sides. The performance was going over perfectly because everybody wanted so much to believe it—going over perfectly, that is, with everyone but the central figure of the tragedy. He was not deceived. Neither apparently was Gatti, who, twenty years later, confessed in his memoirs that the first collapse in Brooklyn had filled him with grave forebodings. "At that very moment," he said, "I had a fleeting premonition that Caruso was lost."

Annie Kempter was not fooled either. Annie was head of the cleaning women and dared sound the only baleful note. What she beheld crushed her and she couldn't hold it back.

"Mr. Caruso," she whispered, "I think you look terrible."

"Annie," Caruso replied quietly, "you are the only one who tells me the truth."

With Mrs. Caruso and Gloria he sailed from Brooklyn on the *Presidente Wilson.* There was a great turnout and general merrymaking on the pier.

The rooms the Carusos occupied at the Hotel Vittoria in Sorrento are pretty much today as they were then except that the great gilt piano is gone. Undeterred by the heavy blinds, the sunlight and salt air have faded the ornate damask covering the walls. The overblown Louis XVI furniture is the same.

Enrico swam every day, Gloria never far from his side. He found his way through the Vittoria's gardens to the beautiful little town square. Everywhere he was greeted like a king. He was gaining weight as his photographs show and he was gorgeously tanned. But he foolishly insisted on making trips to Capri and Pompeii.

On July 15, he felt the old pain in his side. It was July 28 before he would consent to see the famous Bastianelli brothers, the best doctors in Italy at the time. Their verdict was that a kidney must be removed. The operation would be done at their clinic in Rome the next week. Two days later Caruso sank into delirium. Mrs. Caruso called Giovanni and the sad little party set forth, deciding to break the journey in Naples. They checked into the Hotel Vesuvio. The end was swift and terrible, in indescribable heat and pain. He began to scream again, those same dreadful cries of Christmas Day.

Tuesday morning, August 2, Mrs. Caruso remembered hearing the clock strike nine. In the next five minutes he spoke three times.

"Doro—I—am—thirsty."

"Doro—they—hurt—me—again."

"Doro—I—can't—get—my—breath."

That was all.

‡ Their stepmother, Maria Castaldi Caruso. See page 146.

I am often asked, "What did Caruso die of?" The letter to his brother is a painfully accurate medical history. Several of the doctors Mrs. Caruso never forgave, particularly him of the inter-costal neuralgia diagnosis. She also had some definite ideas about the Neapolitan practitioners who couldn't be roused those awful first days of August or who, when finally rounded up, were so over-whelmed by the celebrity of their patient as to be completely ineffectual.

Mr. Gatti said, "He was truly a victim of his own wilfulness." He might have said of his own fear of doctors. "He listened to the conflicting advice of many physicians and even to charlatans. And then it was too late."

Claudia Cassidy is perhaps nearest the truth when she writes, ". . . in his fierce striving to be more than his public expected he was his own executioner. . . ." And, again, he was "a warrior to whom every performance was a battle against the supreme odds of his own previous triumphs. . . ."

Always the tantalizing question raises itself, "What if he had lived?" He was forty-eight and at the height of his powers. When asked at what age the singing voice is best he once said, "For tenors I think between thirty and forty-five." But a healthy Caruso could easily have gone on another ten years at the top. "Indeed," Irving Kolodin speculates, "with his power and endurance, he might have passed sixty still vocally hale."

And what if he had survived the illness? One of his doctors told Mr. Gatti, "Caruso will per-haps pull through, and he will keep his voice, for the voice has nothing to do with pleurisy. But this man will never again have the necessary breath with all these operations."

Caruso had his wife and baby to live for. More than once in his adorable letters to his young wife he expressed a longing to retire. But the most beloved singer of all time not singing? One remembers the entry Yeats made in his diary a few days after the death, at thirty-seven, of J. M. Synge:

"We pity the living and not such dead as he. He has gone upward out of his ailing body into the heroical fountains. We are parched by time."

The Carusos' last New York home was the Vanderbilt Hotel (below). Their suite on the top floor left was the one Alfred Gwynne Vanderbilt set aside for himself and occupied until he perished on the *Lusitania*. During his illness, Caruso later wrote his brother, his screams of pain could be heard in the street eighteen floors below.

East Hampton, L. I.

Agosto 3 -1920

Caro Zirato

Qui accluso trove
ai cheque per
spese che facesti.
tanto ti ringrazio.
Articoli - non Vado
molto di fretta poiche
o solo finito I in

Bruno Zirato

August 3, 1920, a year less a day from his death, Caruso despite illness and unutterable weariness makes a heart-breaking attempt to be his old gay self at the Southampton Fair. In a special booth he makes drawings for charity. The same day he wrote Zirato a letter, a page of which is reproduced above: "I suffer terribly with pains in general," he said. Note the handwriting has lost a good deal of its shape and drive.

At right, the mask of tragedy, the convalescent Caruso.

On April 26, 1921, with Mrs. Caruso and a nurse, he emerges from the hotel for his daily automobile ride in the park, the first photograph since the illness which struck him four months before on Christmas Day.

Pagliaccio again, out for a walk with Mrs. Caruso. "He and his collar of pre-illness days are no longer the close associates they used to be, as he himself demonstrates," says the caption writer, somewhat less deft as a humorist than Caruso, and not nearly so gallant.

142

America's last sight of him, aboard the S. S. *Presidente Wilson,* May 28, 1921.

Widely published as his last photograph in life, Caruso is seen (right) on his balcony at the Vittoria Hotel, Sorrento. The snapshot below, taken on the same balcony with Gloria, may actually be later.

143

Gloria Caruso

Santa Lucia in Naples. How often Caruso sang its beauties; how much more often in the long New York winters he must have longed for them. In the Vesuvio Hotel, at far left, he breathed his last. The window between the two dots is the room. The hotel was bombed during the war but was handsomely rebuilt.

The great man in death, August 3, 1921. The salon of the Vesuvio became his death chapel. The whole world mourned.

144

The funeral procession moves along Santa Lucia from the Vesuvio to the Church of San Francesco di Paola, across the Piazza Plebiscito from the Royal Palace and the San Carlo Opera House. Below: The clergy headed by the metropolitan of Naples leaves the church. A royal basilica, San Francesco di Paola, had never been the scene of any but royal weddings, baptisms and funerals. The King of Italy himself opened the church for Caruso. "I alone in all the city could not feel the weight of this solemn honor," Mrs. Caruso wrote. "There had been many kings but only one Caruso."

145

The caretaker shows an American sailor Caruso's tomb. Del Pianto Cemetery lies on a cypress-shaded hill overlooking Naples. You pass it on the way from the airport into the city. Thousands of visitors make their way here each year. It was not until 1929 that Mrs. Caruso succeeded in getting the coffin closed.

After his death his stepmother listens to one of his records. She was gentle and patient, and Caruso loved her to the end. It always disturbed him that despite his repeated urgings she continued to live on modestly in Naples.

Official Nato-South Photo

Wide World Photos

Mrs. Caruso and Edward Johnson, general manager of the Metropolitan, with the silver bust which Mrs. Caruso gave the opera house in 1947. It stands in the foyer of the family circle. Right: Rudolf Bing, general manager of the Metropolitan since 1950, at the heroic bronze bust of the singer which used to dominate the main lobby of the historic theater.

Photo by Edward Steichen. Reprinted from Vanity Fair. ©*1935, Conde Nast.*

". . . Caruso is as urgent in communication as if he had closed the door of a room, not of life," says Claudia Cassidy of the *Chicago Tribune.* "A dozen years after his death Clifford Odets used the swelling splendors of *O Paradiso* to symbolize the vicarious release from frustration in *Awake and Sing."* The phonograph was offstage but Steichen's wonderful photograph is an apotheosis of the play and, in a way, also of Caruso. As his voice pours forth, a transfigured Bronx patriarch quotes the exhortation and prophecy of Isaiah, "Awake and sing, ye that dwell in dust, and the earth shall cast out the dead."

CARUSO DISCOGRAPHY

BY

JOHN SECRIST

Appearing originally in *The Record Collector* in 1951, this discography was the first on Caruso to be based upon complete information from Victor files. In the present version, some needed modifications have been attended to, and recent catalog numbers have been added.

Ordinarily, when an artist first recorded a given selection for Victor, a new "matrix number" was assigned, and then subsequent versions of the same selection were assigned the same matrix number, followed after a hyphen by different "take numbers." In this listing, "discography numbers" have been assigned to all "published" versions (those which exist with a catalog number embossed on the record surface), to all unpublished titles, and to other unpublished takes involving artists not on the published versions. The remaining unpublished takes are listed under the corresponding published versions.

Note that the titles as given here may differ from those found on certain editions of the records. Operatic selections are listed in the order in which they occur in the opera. The composer is given after the title, or in a neighboring listing from the same opera. Additional artists are then given, followed by the language if this is other than Italian or its dialects. Where these specifications fail to distinguish between different versions of the same selection, additional designations are included.

Below the title line are two "categories" of information, separated by a period. The first category is devoted to catalog numbers, which are separated by semicolons into "classes." Each class is prefaced by an "identification," set apart by a colon. Each identification is defined as implying all classifications containing it in the following outline:

Laterally cut discs:
  "33"–33 1/3 r.p.m.
  "45"–45 r.p.m.
  78 r.p.m.:
    "RR"–Rerecordings with new orchestra
    Editions with original orchestra:
      "RI"–Reissues (after significant deletion)
      Originals (before significant deletion)
        "Ger" –German nos., incl. Opera Disc
        "HMV"–Eur. pressings from Am. masters
        "V"   –Am. pressings from Am. masters
        "Mon" –Am. pressings from Eur. masters
        "G&T" –Eur. pressings from Eur. masters
        "Zon" –Zonophone
    Earliest lateral transcriptions of AICCs:
      "Herrold"
      "CRS" –Collectors' Record Shop
Vertically cut discs transcribed from AICCs:
  "Emerson"
  "Pathé"
"AICC"–Anglo-Italian Commerce Co. cylinders

Following each identification, and separated by commas, are the corresponding catalog numbers, each possibly followed by parenthetic information pertaining to the individual number. For the 78 r.p.m. classes, single-faced numbers stand alone, and double-faced numbers are each followed by reference to the reverse ("r") side, which is specified by discography number if it is by Caruso. Similarly for "45" numbers having a single selection by Caruso on each side, but otherwise these stand alone, as do all "33" numbers. Following the word "in," however, will be the number of a containing album or set. LCT-6701 and LM-6127 are "33" sets, whose individual records are differentiated by appended digits. Note that following the identification of a class (recognizable by its subsequent colon), the symbols "V" and "HMV" merely signify the label, without the above connotations. For each record, the first number given is that of the "absolute" original. "Pirated" 78 r.p.m. transcriptions like "Pan-American" are disregarded.

Following the period which terminates the category of catalog numbers is a category of matrix numbers and dates. The AICCs and Zonophones have no special matrix numbers, the G&Ts have purely numerical matrix numbers, and those for the Victors are prefixed by a letter. 78 r.p.m. sizes are determinate from the matrix numbers, since the AICC transcriptions, Zonophones, and G&Ts are 10″ except for 12″ #186, and of the Victors, "B" signifies 10″ and "C" 12″, except for duly marked RRs. For the AICCs and Zonophones, the second category gives only the recording dates, reasoned to be subsequent to the 1900 and 1902 premières of TOSCA and GERMANIA, respectively. Elsewhere, each matrix number is followed by the recording date in parentheses, with slants separating month, day, and year, or month and year, in that order. For multiple-take Victors, this information is given first for the published take, followed after a semicolon by similar information for the unpublished takes, separated by commas. But after the recording date of the published take, "listed" dates are also usually given. These specify the durations of the original "V" or "Mon" numbers in domestic Victor catalogs. Slants are included in date designations, hyphens connect dates which specify inclusion in catalogs, and commas similarly mark deletion intervals. Stipulation of the century ("19") denotes a calendar year rather than a specific catalog. Victor labels possessed by a record can be inferred from its listed dates as follows:

1903-3/05 –Monarch (10″) and De Luxe (12″)
4/05-5/09 –Grand Prize
5/09-12/13 –Patents
1/14-10/17 –No Patents ("Victor")
10/17-1933 –"Victrola"
1933   –Orthophonic (1437 and 7156 only)
1934-1941 –"Victor" acoustic-style label
1941-9/54 –Dull-red electric-style label

An "S/8" after the listed dates indicates that from about 1917 on, pressings were made from a transcribed master, so marked. Note that while absence of catalog numbers indicates that a record is strictly unpublished, absence of listed dates indicates merely that the record did not appear with standard Victor labels.

1. *Addio* (Tosti)
V: 88280, 6021 (r:168), 7156 (r:6); HMV:
2-052035, DB 131 (r:168), DB 1386 (r:6);
Ger: 76096, 85027 (r:229); RR: HMV DB 3327
(r:182); 45: V Christmas gift 1951 (r:266).
C-9747 (12/29/10) (2/11-28,30-33)

2. *Addio a Napoli, L'* (Cottrau)
V: 87312, 502 (r:44); HMV: 7-52159,
DA 104 (r:44); RR: V 2212 (r:168),
HMV DA 1655 (r:168); 45: V 17-0133 (r:61).
B-23140-6 (9/9/19) (9/20-40); B-23140-1,2,3
(9/8/19), B-23140-4,5 (9/9/19)

3. *Adorables tourments* (Barthélemy) (in French)
V: 88115, 6006 (r:56); HMV: 032070,
DB 116 (r:56); Ger: 76014, 85005 (r:246).
C-5009 (1/10/08) (5/08-26,4/27)

4. ADRIANA LECOUVREUR: *No, più nobile* (Cilèa)
G&T: 52419; 33: Rococo 2, FRP 5.
2880 (11/02)

5. AFRICANA: *O paradiso* (Meyerbeer)
V: 88054, 6007 (r:48); HMV: 052157,
DB 117 (r:48); Ger: 76072, 85015 (r:48);
RR: V 14234 (r:48), HMV DB 2991 (r:220);
45: V 17-0051 (r:49) (in WCT-11);
33: V LCT-1007, HMV FJLP-5009, V LM-6127-34.
C-4160-2 (2/20/07) (3/07-28,30) (S/8);
C-4160-1 (12/30/06)

6. AFRICANA: *Deh, ch'io ritorni* (Meyerbeer)
V: 7156 (r:1); HMV: DB 1386 (r:1);
RI: HMV AGSB 18 (r:79); 33: V LCT-6701-3.
C-24464-5 (9/16/20) (1/30-33);
C-24464-1,2,3 (9/15/20), C-24464-4 (9/16/20)

7. *Agnus Dei* (Bizet) (in Latin)
V: 88425, 6010 (r:163); HMV: 02470,
DB 120 (r:163); Ger: 76002, 85003 (r:120);
RI: V 11-0035 (r:60) (in DM 1359);
RR: V 17814 (r:116), HMV DB 2644 (r:234);
45: V 17-0036 (in WCT-8); 33: V LCT-1005.
C-12942 (2/24/13) (5/13-28,30)

8. *A Granada* (Alvarez) (in Spanish)
V: 88623, 6011 (r:42), 8038 (r:20);
HMV: 2-062007, DB 592 (r:20); RR: V 17-5001
(r:171) (10"), V 26571 (r:171) (10"); 45: V
17-0336 (r:241) (in WCT-35); 33: V LCT-1034.
C-22124-3 (9/26/18) (11/20-33);
C-22124-1 (7/10/18), C-22124-2 (9/26/18)

9. *Ah luna* (Varel)
B-15571-1,2 (1/7/15)

10. AIDA: *Celeste Aida* (final note sung softly)
G&T: 52369. 1784 (3/02)

11. AIDA: *Celeste Aida* (final phrase omitted)
G&T: 52369, HMV DA 549 (r:94); Mon: 5008,
91007; Ger: 74514; RI: HMV VA 12 (r:75).
2873 (11/02) (03-9/07)

12. AIDA: *Celeste Aida* (with piano)
V: 85022; HMV: 052074.
C-997 (2/1/04) (4/04-7/09)

13. AIDA: *Celeste Aida* (crescendo on final note)
V: 88025. C-3180-1 (3/13/06)

14. AIDA: *Celeste Aida* (without recitative)
V: 88127; HMV: 052224, DB 144 (r:216);
Ger: 76080, 78512 (r:37), 85020 (r:55).
C-3180-3 (3/29/08) (7/08-1912);
C-3180-2 (3/29/08)

15. AIDA: *Celeste Aida* (with recitative)
V: 88127, 6000 (r:97); HMV: 2-052066,
DK 115 (r:16); Ger: 76108, 85022 (r:97);
RR: V 7770 (r:187), HMV DB 1875 (r:187),
V 8993 (r: Ponselle- Ritorna) (in M 303),
V 12-1014 (r:77) (in DM 1329);
45: V 17-0053 (r:123) (in WCT-11),
V 17-0129 (r:111), V ERAT-6;
33: V LCT-1007, HMV FJLP-5009, V LM-6127-16.
C-11423 (12/27/11) (1912-9/52)

16. AIDA: *Già i sacerdoti adunansi* (with Homer)
V: 89050, 8012 (r:17); HMV: 2-054015,
DK 115 (r:15); Ger: 78522, 78522 (r:17);
RI: V 15-1025 (r:17);
45: V 17-0341 (in WCT-51); 33: V LCT-1035.
C-9748 (12/29/10) (3/11-28)

17. AIDA: *Aida a me togliesti* (with Homer)
V: 89051, 8012 (r:16); HMV: 2-054016,
2-054094, DM 111 (r:63); Ger: 78523,
78522 (r:16); RI: V 15-1025 (r:16);
45: V 17-0340 (in WCT-51); 33: V LCT-1035.
C-9749 (12/29/10) (3/11-28)

18. AIDA: *La fatal pietra* (Verdi) (with Gadski)
V: 89028, 8015 (r:19); HMV: 2-054005,
DM 114 (r:19); Ger: 78516, 78516 (r:19).
C-8353 (11/7/09) (1/10-28,30)

19. AIDA: *O terra, addio* (Verdi) (with Gadski)
V: 89029, 8015 (r:18); HMV: 2-054006,
DM 114 (r:18); Ger: 78517, 78516 (r:18).
C-8348-2 (11/6/09) (1/10-28,30);
C-8348-1 (11/6/09)

20. *A la luz de la luna* (Michelena)
(with De Gogorza) (in Spanish)
V: 89083, 8038 (r:8); HMV: 2-064001,
DB 592 (r:8); RI: HMV VB 58 (r:184);
33: V LM-6127-25. C-21773-2 (4/16/18)
(7/18-30); C-21773-1 (4/16/18)

21. *Alba separa dalla luce l'ombra, L'* (Tosti)
V: 87272, 503 (r:165); HMV: 7-52104,
DA 121 (r:177); RI: HMV VA 40 (r:170);
33: V LCT-1129. B-19484-2 (4/15/17)
(7/17-28); B-19484-1 (4/15/17)

22. AMADIS: *Bois épais* (Lully) (in French)
V: 1437 (r:195); HMV: DA 1097 (r:195);
RI: HMV AGSA 27 (r:195); 33: V LM-6127-25.
B-24465-6 (9/16/20) (1/30-11/18/32);
B-24465-1,2,3,4 (9/15/20), B-24465-5 (9/16/20)

23. *Amor mio* (Ricciardi)
V: 87176, 504 (r:58); HMV: 7-52055,
DA 105 (r:58); Ger: 74545, 80019 (r:124);
RI: HMV VA 45 (r:58); 33: V LCT-1129.
B-14356 (1/21/14) (4/14-28)

24. ANDREA CHÉNIER: *Un dì all'azzurro spazio*
(Giordano)
V: 88060, 6008 (r:55); HMV: 052158, DB 700
(r:65); Ger: 76073; 85016 (r:111). C-4316
(3/17/07) (5/07-33); C-4161 (12/30/06)

25. ANDREA CHÉNIER: *Come un bel dì di maggio*
    V: 87266, 516 (r:53); HMV: 7-52094, DA 117
    (r:53). B-18659 (11/3/16) (12/17-27,30-33)

26. *Ave Maria* (Gounod) (acc. Kreisler) (in Latin)
    C-14664 (4/3/14)

27. *Ave Maria* (Kahn) (acc. Elman) (in Latin)
    V: 89065, 8007 (r:71); HMV: 02472, DK 103
    (r:71); Ger: 77500, 85045 (r:71); 45: V
    17-0033 (r:265) (in WCT-7), V 17-0127 (r:96),
    V 449-0013 (in WCT-1121); 33: V LCT-2,
    V LCT-1121, HMV QKLP-501, HMV FKLP-7001.
    C-13004-1 (3/20/13) (6/13-9/51);
    C-13004-2,3 (3/20/13)

28. *Bacio ancora, Un* (Trimarchi)
    Zon: X-1550; 33: Scala 825. (1902)

29. BALLO IN MASCHERA: *La rivedrò nell'estasi*
    (with Hempel, Rothier, De Segurola)
    V: 89077, 10005 (r:31); HMV: 2-054052,
    DM 103 (r:31). C-14659-2 (4/3/14)
    (8/14-28,30); C-14659-1 (4/3/14)

30. BALLO IN MASCHERA: *Dì tu se fedele* (Verdi)
    V: 87091, 512 (r:250); HMV: 7-52025, DA 102
    (r:204); Ger: 74532, 80009 (r:204); 45: V
    17-0335 (r:163) (in WCT-35); 33: V LCT-1034.
    B-11270-2 (11/19/11) (12/11-28,30);
    B-11270-1 (11/19/11)

31. BALLO IN MASCHERA: *È scherzo od è follia*
    (with Hempel, Duchene, Rothier, De Segurola)
    V: 89076, 10005 (r:29); HMV: 2-054050,
    DM 103 (r:29); RI: V 16-5000 (r:132) (in
    M 953); 45: V 17-0018 (r:253) (in WCT-4),
    V ERAT-8; 33: V LCT-1003. C-14660-1
    (4/3/14) (6/14-28,30); C-14660-2 (4/3/14)

32. BALLO IN MASCHERA: *Ma se m'è forza perderti*
    V: 88346, 6027 (r:221); HMV: 2-052065,
    DB 137 (r:221); Ger: 76107, 85031 (r:221).
    C-11420 (12/27/11) (1/13-28)

33. *Because* (D'Hardelot) (in French)
    V: 87122, 506 (r:115); HMV: 7-32004,
    DA 107 (r:115); Ger: 74503, 80002 (r:193),
    80020 (r:114); RR: V 1688 (r:165),
    HMV DA 1380 (r:165); 45: V 17-0032 (r:96)
    (in WCT-7); 33: V LCT-2, HMV QKLP-501,
    HMV FKLP-7001. B-12680-2 (12/7/12)
    (2/13-26,4/27); B-12680-1 (12/7/12)

34. BOHÈME: *Io non ho che una povera stanzetta*
    V: 88335, 6012 (r:35); HMV: 2-052061,
    DB 122 (r:35); Ger: 76104, 85028 (r:35);
    RI: V 15-1038 (r:139).
    C-11276 (11/26/11) (2/12-28)

35. BOHÈME: *Testa adorata* (Leoncavallo)
    V: 88331, 6012 (r:34); HMV: 2-052059,
    DB 122 (r:34); Ger: 76102, 85028 (r:34);
    45: V 17-0337 (r:262) (in WCT-35); 33: V
    LCT-1034. C-11272 (11/19/11) (12/11-28)

36. BOHÈME: *Che gelida manina* (Puccini)
    V: 88002, 6003 (r:125); HMV: 052122,
    DB 113 (r:110); Ger: 76066, 85012 (r:77);
    45: V 17-0052 (r:187) (in WCT-11), V ERAT-5;
    33: V LCT-1007, HMV FJLP-5009, V LM-6127-34.
    C-3101 (2/11/06) (5/06-40)

37. BOHÈME: *O soave fanciulla* (with Melba)
    V: 95200; HMV: 054129;
    Ger: 78512, 78512 (r:14); 33: V LCT-6701-1.
    C-4326-1 (3/24/07) (5/07-26,4/27);
    C-4326-2 (3/24/07), C-4326-3,4 (4/1/07)

38. BOHÈME: *O soave fanciulla* (with Farrar)
    V: IRCC 61 (r:186);
    RI: HMV AGSB 50 (r: Farrar, Jacoby- Tutti);
    33: V LM-6127-34. C-12751-1 (12/30/12);
    C-11617-1,2 (2/27/12), C-12751-2 (12/30/12)

39. BOHÈME: *Addio, dolce svegliare* (Puccini)
    (with Farrar, Viafora, Scotti)
    V: 96002, 10007 (r: Farrar- Mimi! Speravo);
    HMV: 054204, DO 101 (r: Farrar- Hirondelles);
    Ger: 79002, 79001 (r:211); RI: V 16-5001
    (r:211) (in M 953). C-6025 (3/10/08) (5/08-30)

40. BOHÈME: *Ah Mimi, tu più non torni* (w. Scotti)
    V: 89006, 8000 (r:98); HMV: 054127,
    DM 105 (r:98); Ger: 78511, 78510 (r:98).
    C-4315 (3/17/07) (5/07-48)

41. BOHÈME: *Vecchia zimarra, senti* (Puccini)
    V: 87499 (r: Alda, Butterworth- Dialogue);
    HMV: DL 100 (r: Alda, Butterworth- Dialogue).
    B-17198 (2/23/16)

42. *Campana di San Giusto, La* (Arona)
    V: 88612, 6011 (r:8); HMV: 2-052153, DB 616
    (r:113); 33: V LM-6127-16. C-22514-1
    (1/6/19) (9/19-33); C-22514-2 (1/6/19)

43. *Campane a sera* (Malfetti)
    V: 88615, 6024 (r:190); HMV: 2-052177,
    DB 134 (r:190). C-22259-3 (9/26/18)
    (4/20-28,30); C-22259-1,2 (9/26/18)

44. *Canta pe' me* (De Curtis)
    V: 87092, 502 (r:2); HMV: 7-52026,
    DA 104 (r:2); Ger: 74533, 80016 (r:191).
    B-11306-2 (11/26/11) (2/12-40);
    C-9746 (12/29/10), B-11306-1 (11/26/11)

45. *Cantique de Noël* (Adam) (in French)
    V: 88561, 6029 (r:219); HMV: 2-032022,
    DB 139 (r:219); 45: V 449-0013
    (in WCT-1121); 33: V LCT-1121. C-17218-3
    (2/23/16) (11/16-28); C-17218-1,2 (2/23/16)

46. CARMEN: *Parle-moi de ma mère* (w. Alda) (in Fr.)
    V: 89083 (number later assigned to 20).
    C-15483-3 (12/10/14); C-15483-1,2 (12/10/14)

47. CARMEN: *Flower song* (Bizet) (with piano)
    V: 85049; HMV: 052087; RI: HMV VB 57
    (r:118). C-2341 (2/27/05) (5/05-7/09)

48. CARMEN: *Flower song* (Bizet) (in Italian)
    V: 88209, 6007 (r:5); HMV: 2-052007,
    DB 117 (r:5); Ger: 76092, 85015 (r:5);
    RR: V 14234 (r:5), HMV DB 3023 (r:55),
    V 12-1016 (r:55) (in DM 1329).
    C-8349 (11/7/09) (12/09-28,30)

49. CARMEN: *Flower song* (Bizet) (in French)
    V: 88208, 6004 (r:81); HMV: 2-032000,
    DB 130 (r:148); Ger: 76015, 85006 (r:186);
    45: V 17-0051 (r:5) (in WCT-11),
    V 17-0128 (r:250), V ERAT-7;
    33: V LCT-1007, HMV FJLP-5009, V LM-6127-34.
    C-8350 (11/7/09) (12/09-28,30-33)

50. CAVALLERIA RUSTICANA: *Siciliana* (Zonophone)
Zon: X-1556; 33: Rococo 2, Scala 825. (1902)

51. CAVALLERIA RUSTICANA: *Siciliana* (G&T)
G&T: 52418, HMV DA 545 (r:54);
Mon: 5012, 91011; RI: HMV VA 30 (r:178).
2876 (11/02) (03 only)

52. CAVALLERIA RUSTICANA· *Siciliana* (with piano)
V: 81030, 521 (r:54); HMV: 52064.
B-1000 (2/1/04) (4/04-11/16,22-24,6/25)

53. CAVALLERIA RUSTICANA: *Siciliana* (with harp)
V: 87072, 516 (r:25); HMV: 7-52018, DA 117
(r:25); Ger: 74530, 80010 (r:197); 45: V
ERAT-1. B-9745 (12/28/10) (3/11-27,30-33)

54. CAVALLERIA RUSTICANA: *Brindisi* (Mascagni)
V: 81062, 521 (r:52); HMV: 52193,
DA 545 (r:51); Ger: 74513, 80005 (r:147);
RI: HMV VA 33 (r:149).
B-2344 (2/27/05) (5/05-19,22-24,6/25)

55. CAVALLERIA RUSTICANA: *Addio alla madre*
V: 88458, 6008 (r:24); HMV: 2-052083,
DB 118 (r:139); Ger: 76113, 85020 (r:14);
RR: V 15732 (r:198), HMV DB 3023 (r:48),
V 12-1016 (r:48) (in DM 1329); 45: V 17-0365
(in WCT-62); 33: V LCT-1039. C-14202-2
(12/15/13) (2/14-33); C-14202-1 (12/15/13)

56. *Chanson de juin* (Godard) (in French)
V: 88579, 6006 (r:3); HMV: 2-032027,
DB 116 (r:3); RI: HMV VB 59 (r:261); 33: V
LCT-1129. C-18658 (11/3/16) (3/17-26,4/27)

57. CID: *O souverain* (Massenet) (in French)
V: 88554, 6013 (r:123); HMV: 2-032025,
DB 123 (r:123); 45: V 17-0339 (r:250)
(in WCT-35); 33: V LCT-1034, V LM-6127-34.
C-17122-2 (2/5/16) (8/16-28,30);
C-17122-1 (2/5/16)

58. *Cielo turchino* (Ciociano)
V: 87218, 504 (r:23); HMV: 7-52073,
DA 105 (r:23); RI: HMV VA 45 (r:23);
33: V LCT-1129. B-15569 (1/7/15) (10/15-28)

59. *Core 'ngrato* (Cardillo)
V: 88334, 6032 (r:220); HMV: 2-052060,
DB 142 (r:220); Ger: 76103, 85029 (r:95).
C-11274 (11/19/11) (12/11-33)

60. *Crucifix* (Faure) (with Journet) (in French)
V: 89054, 6347 (r: Plançon- Rameaux);
HMV: 2-034013, DB 591 (r: Plançon- Rameaux);
Ger: 78504, 78504 (r: Plançon- Rameaux);
RI: V 11-0035 (r:7) (in DM 1359).
C-11442 (1/7/12) (3/12-24,6/25)

61. *Danza, La* (Rossini)
V: 88355, 6031 (r:231); HMV: 2-052068,
DB 141 (r:231); Ger: 76110, 85035 (r:231);
RI: V 15-1040 (r:95); 45: V 17-0133 (r:2).
C-11590 (2/13/12) (5/12-28,5/19/33-5/34)

62. *Deux sérénades, Les* (Leoncavallo)
(accompanied by Elman) (in French)
V: 89085, 8008 (r:228); HMV: 2-032017,
DK 104 (r:228); 33: V LM-6127-35. C-15683-2
(2/6/15) (5/15-30); C-15683-1 (2/6/15)

63. DON CARLOS: *Dio, che nell'alma infondere*
(Verdi) (with Scotti)
V: 89064, 8036 (r:185); HMV: 2-054043,
2-054095, DM 111 (r:17); Ger: 78533,
78533 (r:176). C-12752 (12/30/12) (4/13-28)

64. DON PASQUALE: *Com'è gentil* (Donizetti)
V: 85048, 6036 (r:110); HMV: 052086,
DB 159 (r:156); RI: HMV VB 55 (r:183).
C-2340 (2/27/05) (5/05-19,22-24,6/25)

65. DON SEBASTIANO: *Deserto in terra* (Donizetti)
(three descending pairs of notes after
orchestral anticipation of opening words)
V: 88106, 6014 (r:139); HMV: 052209,
DB 700 (r:24); Ger: 76078, 85010 (r:93).
C-5008-1 (1/10/08) (3/08-24,6/25)

66. DON SEBASTIANO: *Deserto in terra* (Donizetti)
(lacking pairs of notes described above)
V: 15-1037 (r:119); 33: V LM-6127-25.
C-5008-2 (1/10/08) (11/48-9/49)

67. *Dopo* (Tosti)
C-22126-1,2,3 (7/11/18)

68. *Dream, A* (Bartlett) (in English)
V: 87321, 507 (r:96); HMV: DA 108 (r:96);
RR: V S-1617, V 1658 (r:96), HMV DA 1349
(r:96). B-24466-3 (9/16/20) (2/21-33);
B-24466-1 (9/15/20), B-24466-2 (9/16/20)

69. *Dreams of long ago* (Caruso) (in English)
V: 88376, 6015 (r:130); HMV: 02396,
DB 125 (r:130); Ger: 76000, 85001 (r:128);
45: V 449-0009 (in WCT-1112); 33:
V LCT-1112. C-11616-3 (4/18/12) (7/12-30);
C-11616-1 (2/27/12), C-11616-2 (4/18/12)

70. DUCA D'ALBA: *Angelo casto e bel* (Donizetti)
V: 88516, 6355 (r:113); HMV: 2-052101,
DB 640 (r:121); RI: HMV VB 56 (r:167).
C-15572-2 (1/7/15) (7/15-28,30);
C-15572-1 (1/7/15)

71. *Élégie* (Massenet) (acc. Elman) (in French)
V: 89066, 8007 (r:27); HMV: 2-032010,
DK 103 (r:27); Ger: 77502, 85045 (r:27);
45: V 17-0031 (r:128) (in WCT-7);
33: V LCT-2, HMV QKLP-501, HMV FKLP-7001.
C-13005-1 (3/20/13) (10/13-9/51);
C-13005-2,3 (3/20/13)

72. ELISIR D'AMORE: *Venti scudi* (Donizetti)
(with De Luca)
V: 89089, 8006 (r:99); HMV: 2-054092,
DM 107 (r:99); 33: V LM-6127-25. C-22576-2
(2/10/19) (11/19-28,30); C-22576-1 (2/10/19)

73. ELISIR D'AMORE: *Una furtiva lagrima* (Zon.)
Zon: X-1552; 33: Rococo 2, Scala 825. (1902)

74. ELISIR D'AMORE: *Una furtiva lagrima* (G&T)
G&T: 52346. 1786 (3/02)

75. ELISIR D'AMORE: *Una furtiva lagrima* (part 1)
V: 81027, 930 (r:179); HMV: 52065;
RI: HMV VA 12 (r:11); 33: V LM-6127-25.
B-996 (2/1/04) (4/04-19)

76. ELISIR D'AMORE: *Una furtiva lagrima* (part 2)
V: 85021; HMV: 052073; RI: HMV VB 16
(rerecording) (r: Giorgini- De' miei),
HMV VB 44 (original master) (r:186).
C-996 (2/1/04) (4/04-1/07)

77. ELISIR D'AMORE: *Una furtiva lagrima* (orch.)
V: 88339, 6016 (r:205); HMV: 2-052064,
DB 126 (r:205); Ger: 76106, 85012 (r:36);
RR: V 11-8112 (r:205), HMV DB 3903 (r:205),
V 12-1014 (r:15) (in DM 1329);
45: V 17-0049 (r:208) (in WCT-11), V 17-0131
(r:205); 33: V LCT-1007, HMV FJLP-5009.
C-996 (11/26/11) (3/12-3/52)

78. *Eternamente* (Mascheroni)
V: 88333, 6034 (r:216); HMV: 2-052058,
DB 121 (r:144); Ger: 76161, 85042 (r:125);
RI: HMV VB 60 (r:125).
C-11271 (11/19/11) (12/11-28)

79. EUGEN ONEGIN: *Echo lointain de ma jeunesse*
(Tchaikovsky) (in French)
V: 88582, 6017 (r:169); HMV: 2-032028,
DB 127 (r:169); RI: HMV AGSB 18 (r:6).
C-18657-1 (11/3/16) (6/17-26,4/27);
C-18657-2 (11/3/16)

80. FAUST: *O merveille* (with Journet) (in French)
V: 89039, 8016 (r:151); HMV: 2-034000,
DM 115 (r:151); Ger: 78537, 78519 (r:151);
45: V 449-0132 (r:92) (in WCT-1103);
33: V LCT-1103. C-8555-2 (1/16/10)
(4/10-26,4/27); C-8555-1 (1/16/10)

81. FAUST: *Salut, demeure chaste et pure* (in French)
V: 88003, 6004 (r:49); HMV: 032030,
DK 116 (r:185); Ger: 76013, 85004 (r:148);
45: V 449-0133 (r:86) (in WCT-1103),
V ERAT-7; 33: V LCT-1103.
C-3102 (2/11/06) (5/06-28,30-33) (S/8)

82. FAUST: *Seigneur Dieu* (Gounod) (with
Farrar, Mme. Gilibert, Journet) (in French)
V: 95204, 10004 (r:83); HMV: 2-034003,
DM 102 (r:83); Ger: 78500, 78500 (r:83);
45: V 449-0135 (r:83) (in WCT-1103); 33:
V LCT-1103. C-8544 (1/12/10) (5/10-26,4/27)

83. FAUST: *Eh quoi, toujours seule?* (with
Farrar, Mme. Gilibert, Journet) (in French)
V: 95205, 10004 (r:82); HMV: 2-034004,
DM 102 (r:82); Ger: 78500 (r:82);
45: V 449-0135 (r:82) (in WCT-1103); 33:
V LCT-1103. C-8547 (1/12/10) (5/10-26,4/27)

84. FAUST: *Laisse-moi* (with Farrar) (in French)
V: 89032, 8009 (r:85); HMV: 2-034011,
DM 108 (r:85); Ger: 78502, 78502 (r:85);
45: V 17-0027 (in WCT-6), V 449-0134
(in WCT-1103); 33: V LCT-1004, V LCT-1103,
HMV QJLP-101. C-8533 (1/6/10) (5/10-28)

85. FAUST: *Eternelle* (with Farrar) (in French)
V: 89031, 8009 (r:84); HMV: 2-034012,
DM 108 (r:84); Ger: 78503, 78502 (r:84);
45: V 17-0028 (in WCT-6); 33: V LCT-1004.
C-8534-2 (1/6/10) (5/10-28) (S/8);
C-8534-1 (1/6/10)

86. FAUST: *Elle ouvre sa fenêtre* (with Farrar,
Journet) (in Fr.) (Caruso sings only one word.)
V: 89040, 10008 (r:92), 8022 (r: Farrar-
Hirondelles); HMV: 2-034007, DK 106 (r:92);
45: V 449-0133 (r:81) (in WCT-1103); 33: V
LCT-1103. C-8558 (1/17/10) (5/10-28,30-33)

87. FAUST: *Que voulez-vous, messieurs?* (Gounod)
(with De Gogorza, Vieulle) (in French)
C-6681-1,2 (12/19/08)

88. FAUST: *Que voulez-vous, messieurs?* (Gounod)
(with Scotti, Journet) (in French)
V: 95206, 10011 (r:209); HMV: 2-034001,
DO 100 (r:209); Ger: 78539, 78539 (r:127).
C-8556 (1/16/10) (6/10-24,6/25) (S/8)

89. FAUST: *Mon coeur est pénétré d'épouvante*
(Gounod) (with Farrar) (in French)
V: 89033, 8010 (r:90); HMV: 2-034005,
DM 109 (r:90); Ger: 78535, 78535 (r:90).
C-8542-2 (1/12/10) (3/10-26,4/27);
C-8542-1 (1/12/10)

90. FAUST: *Attends, voici la rue*
(Gounod) (with Farrar) (in French)
V: 89034, 8010 (r:89); HMV: 2-034006,
DM 109 (r:89); Ger: 78536, 78535 (r:89).
C-8543-2 (1/12/10) (3/10-26,4/27);
C-8543-1 (1/12/10)

91. FAUST: *Alerte, ou vous êtes perdus* (Gounod)
(with Farrar, Vieulle) (in French)
C-6679-1,2 (12/19/08)

92. FAUST: *Alerte, ou vous êtes perdus* (Gounod)
(with Farrar, Journet) (in French)
V: 95203, 10008 (r:86); HMV: 2-034002,
DK 106 (r:86); Ger: 78538, 77515 (r:
Farrar- Church Scene 1); RI: V 16-5003
(r:217) (in M 953); 45: V 449-0132 (r:80)
(in WCT-1103), V ERAT-8; 33: V LCT-1103.
C-8545-4 (1/16/10) (3/10-28,30-33) (S/8);
C-8545-1,2 (1/12/10), C-8545-3 (1/16/10)

93. FAVORITA: *Spirto gentil* (Donizetti)
V: 88004, 6005 (r:119); HMV: 052120,
DB 129 (r:120); Ger: 76064, 85010 (r:65);
RI: V 15-1036 (r:156); 33: V LCT-6701-1.
C-3104 (2/11/06) (5/06-28,30-33)

94. FEDORA: *Amor ti vieta* (Giordano)
G&T: 52439, HMV DA 549 (r:11);
RI: HMV VA 53 (r:158), HMV VA 58 (r:146);
33: V LM-6127-34. 2872 (11/02)

95. *Fenesta che lucive* (attributed to Bellini)
V: 88439, 6019 (r:120); HMV: 2-052077,
DB 140 (r:246); Ger: 76112, 85029 (r:59);
RI: V 15-1040 (r:61); 33: V LM-6127-25.
C-13107-2 (4/10/13) (11/13-24,6/25);
C-13107-1 (4/10/13)

96. *For you alone* (Geehl) (in English)
V: 87070, 507 (r:68); HMV: 4-2122,
DA 108 (r:68); Ger: 74500, 80000 (r:129);
RR: V 1658 (r:68), HMV DA 1349 (r:68); 45:
V 17-0032 (r:33) (in WCT-7), V 17-0127
(r:27); 33: V LCT-2, HMV QKLP-501,
HMV FKLP-7001. B-9744-1 (12/28/10)
(2/11-33); B-9744-2 (12/28/10)

97. FORZA DEL DESTINO: *O tu che in seno agli angeli*
V: 88207, 6000 (r:15); HMV: 2-052006,
DB 112 (r:249); Ger: 76091, 85022 (r:15);
45: V ERAT-4. C-8345 (11/6/09) (12/09-9/52)

98. FORZA DEL DESTINO: *Solenne in quest'ora*
(Verdi) (with Scotti)
V: 89001, 8000 (r:40); HMV: 054070,
DM 105 (r:40); Ger: 78510, 78510 (r:40);
45: V 17-0026 (in WCT-6), V ERAT-9;
33: V LCT-1004, HMV QJLP-101, V LM-6127-16.
C-3179 (3/13/06) (6/06-48)

99. FORZA DEL DESTINO: *Il segreto fu dunque
violato?* (Verdi) (with De Luca)
V: 89087, 8006 (r:72); HMV: 2-054093,
DM 107 (r:72). C-22123-2 (7/10/18)
(10/18-28,30); C-22123-1 (7/10/18)

100. FORZA DEL DESTINO: *Invano, Alvaro*
(Verdi) (with Amato)
V: 89052, 8005 (r:101); HMV: 2-054027,
DM 106 (r:101); Ger: 78526, 78526 (r:101).
C-11286-2 (11/26/11) (12/11-19,22-28);
C-11286-1 (11/26/11)

101. FORZA DEL DESTINO: *Le minaccie, i fieri
accenti* (Verdi) (with Amato)
V: 89053, 8005 (r:100); HMV: 2-054028,
DM 106 (r:100); Ger: 78527, 78526 (r:100).
C-11286½ (11/26/11) (12/11-28)

102. *Garibaldi's hymn* (Olivieri)
V: 87297, 515 (r:177); HMV: 7-52118,
DA 116 (r:165). B-22260-2 (9/26/18)
(1/19-28); B-22260-1,3 (9/26/18)

103. GERMANIA: *Studenti, udite* (with piano)
G&T: 52378, HMV DA 544 (r:106);
RI: HMV VA 37 (r:106). 1782 (3/02)

104. GERMANIA: *Studenti, udite* (with orchestra)
V: 87053, 508 (r:107); HMV: 7-52013,
DA 543 (r:107); Ger: 74558, 80022 (r:107);
RI: HMV VA 38 (r:107).
B-8710 (3/14/10) (6/10-24,6/25) (S/8)

105. GERMANIA: *No, non chiuder gli occhi vaghi*
(Franchetti) (Zonophone)
Zon: X-1554; 33: Rococo 2, Scala 825. (1902)

106. GERMANIA: *No, non chiuder gli occhi vaghi*
(Franchetti) (with piano)
G&T: 52370, HMV DA 544 (r:103);
RI: HMV VA 37 (r:103). 1788 (3/02)

107. GERMANIA: *No, non chiuder gli occhi vaghi*
(Franchetti) (with orchestra)
V: 87054, 508 (r:104); HMV: 7-52014,
DA 543 (r:104); Ger: 74559, 80022 (r:104);
RI: HMV VA 38 (r:104).
B-8713 (3/14/10) (6/10-24,6/25)

108. GIOCONDA: *Enzo Grimaldo* (with Ruffo)
C-14273 (1/8/14)

109. GIOCONDA: *Cielo e mar* (Ponchielli) (G&T)
G&T: 52417, HMV DA 547 (r:239);
Mon: 5009, 91008; RI: HMV VA 29 (r:239).
2874 (11/02) (03-11/30/04)

110. GIOCONDA: *Cielo e mar* (with piano)
V: 85055, 6036 (r:64);
HMV: 052089, DB 113 (r:36).
C-2343 (2/27/05) (5/05-7/10,22-24,6/25)

111. GIOCONDA: *Cielo e mar* (with orchestra)
V: 88246, 6020 (r:148); HMV: 2-052032,
DB 696 (r:125); Ger: 76094, 85016 (r:24);
45: V 17-0050 (r:180) (in WCT-11),
V 17-0129 (r:15); 33: V LCT-1007,
HMV FJLP-5009, V LM-6127-34.
C-8718 (3/14/10) (9/10-28,30)

112. GIOCONDA: *O sommo Dio* (with Destinn, Homer)
C-17341-1,2 (3/20/16)

113. GUARANY: *Sento una forza indomita*
(Gomez) (with Destinn)
V: 89078, 6355 (r:70); HMV: 2-054053,
DB 616 (r:42). C-14730-1 (4/20/14)
(7/14-28,30); C-14730-2 (4/20/14)

114. *Guardann' a luna* (De Crescenzo)
V: 87162, 509 (r:124); HMV: 7-52043,
DA 106 (r:149); Ger: 74542, 80020 (r:33);
RI: HMV VA 44 (r:191); 33: V LCT-1129.
B-13105-2 (4/10/13) (9/13-26,4/27);
B-13105-1 (4/10/13)

115. *Hantise d'amour* (Szulc) (in French)
V: 87211, 506 (r:33); HMV: 7-32009,
DA 107 (r:33); RI: HMV VA 9 (r:138);
33: V LCT-1129. B-14357-2
(12/10/14) (5/15-11/16,22-26,4/27);
C-14357-1 (1/21/14), C-14357-2 (3/19/14),
B-14357-1 (3/9/14), B-14357-3 (12/10/14)

116. *Hosanna* (Granier) (in French)
V: 88403, 6022 (r:199); HMV: 2-032008,
DB 132 (r:199); Ger: 76018, 85008 (r:199);
RR: V 17814 (r:7), HMV DB 3122 (r:199);
45: V 449-0014 (r:163) (in WCT-1121);
33: V LCT-1121. C-12681-2 (12/7/12)
(2/13-28); C-12681-1 (12/7/12)

117. HUGUENOTS: *Qui sotto il ciel* (Meyerbeer)
AICC: 84006 (cylinder); Pathé: 84006
(single or r: 237 or 260) (vertically cut);
CRS: 6 (r:260); 33: Rare Records M301,
Royale 1595, Royale 1902, FRP 3, Scala 825.
(c.1901)

118. HUGUENOTS: *Bianca al par* (with piano)
V: 85056; HMV: 052088; RI: HMV VB 57 (r:47).
C-2342 (2/27/05) (5/05-7/09,22-23,6/25,4/27)

119. HUGUENOTS: *Bianca al par* (with orchestra)
V: 88210, 6005 (r:93); HMV: 2-052008,
DB 115 (r:261); Ger: 76093, 85011 (r:156);
RI: V 15-1037 (r:66); 45: V 17-0048 (in
WCT-10); 33: V LCT-1006, HMV FJLP-5004.
C-8351 (11/7/09) (12/09-28,30-33)

120. *Ideale* (Tosti)
V: 88049, 6019 (r:95); HMV: 052154,
DB 129 (r:93); Ger: 76071, 85003 (r:7).
C-4162 (12/30/06) (3/07-24,6/25) (S/8)

121. *I' m'arricordo e Napule* (Gioe)
V: 88635, 6009 (r:143); HMV: 2-052198,
DB 640 (r:70); RI: HMV VB 62 (r:227).
C-24462-2 (9/14/20) (8/21-33);
C-24462-1 (9/14/20)

122. IRIS: *Apri la tua finestra* (Mascagni)
G&T: 52368; 33: Rococo 2. 1791 (3/02)

123. JUIVE: *Rachel, quand du Seigneur la gráce tutélaire* (Halévy) (in French)
V: 88625, 6013 (r:57); HMV: 2-032062, DB 123 (r:57); RI: V 15-1004 (r:148); 45: V 17-0053 (r:15) (in WCT-11), V ERAT-26; 33: V LCT-1007, HMV FJLP-5009, V LM-6127-34.
C-24461-2 (9/14/20) (12/20-28,30); C-24461-1 (9/14/20)

124. *Lasciati amar* (Leoncavallo)
V: 87161, 509 (r:114); HMV: 7-52042, DA 113 (r:250); Ger: 74541, 80019 (r:23).
B-13104-2 (4/10/13) (8/13-26,4/27); B-13104-1 (4/10/13)

125. *Lolita* (Buzzi-Peccia)
V: 88120, 6003 (r:36); HMV: 062005, DB 696 (r:111); Ger: 76153, 85042 (r:78); RI: HMV VB 60 (r:78).
C-6032 (3/16/08) (6/08-40) (S/8)

126. LOMBARDI: *La mia letizia infondere* (Verdi)
C-23142-1,2 (9/9/19)

127. LOMBARDI: *Qual voluttà trascorrere* (Verdi)
(with Alda, Journet)
V: 95211, 10010 (r:217); HMV: 2-054029, DM 126 (r:217); Ger: 78542, 78539 (r:88); RI: V 16-5002 (r:155) (in M 953); 33: V LM-6127-25. C-11441 (1/7/12) (3/12-26,4/27)

128. *Lost chord, The* (Sullivan) (in English)
V: 88378, 6023 (r:265); HMV: 02397, DB 133 (r:265); Ger: 76001, 85001 (r:69); RR: V 8806 (r:265), HMV DB 2073 (r:265); 45: V 17-0031 (r:71) (in WCT-7); 33: V LCT-2, HMV QKLP-501, HMV FKLP-7001.
C-11942-1 (4/29/12) (7/12-28,30-33); C-11942-2 (4/29/12)

129. *Love is mine* (Gartner) (in English)
V: 87095, 510 (r:182); HMV: 4-2205, DA 111 (r:192); Ger: 74501, 80000 (r:96).
B-11419-2 (12/27/11) (4/12-24,6/25); B-11419-1 (12/27/11)

130. *Love me or not* (Secchi) (in English)
V: 88616, 6015 (r:69); HMV: 02891, DB 125 (r:69). C-23713-4 (1/29/20) (6/20-30); C-23713-1,2,3 (1/29/20)

131. LUCIA: *Sextet* (Donizetti) (with Sembrich, Severina, Scotti, Journet, Daddi)
V: 96200, 10001 (r:211); HMV: 054205, DQ 101 (r:211); Ger: 79003, 79003 (r:212).
C-5052-4 (2/7/08) (5/08-24,6/25); C-5052-1,2,3 (2/3/08), C-5052-5 (2/7/08)

132. LUCIA: *Sextet* (Donizetti) (with Tetrazzini, Jacoby, Amato, Journet, Bada)
V: 96201; HMV: 2-054034; RI: V 16-5000 (r:31) (in M 953).
C-11446-3 (1/19/12) (4/12-26,4/27); C-11446-1,2 (1/10/12), C-11446-4 (1/19/12)

133. LUCIA: *Sextet* (Donizetti) (with Galli-Curci, Egener, De Luca, Journet, Bada)
V: 95212, 10000 (r:213); HMV: 2-054067, DQ 100 (r:213); 45: V 17-0016 (in WCT-4), V ERAT-8; 33: V LCT-1003, V LM-6127-25.
C-19133-2 (1/25/17) (4/17-9/52); C-19133-1,3 (1/25/17)

134. LUCREZIA BORGIA: *Trio Duchessa* (Donizetti)
(with Destinn, Scotti)
C-14731 (4/20/14)

135. LUISA MILLER: *Quando le sere* (Verdi)
C-8725 (3/14/10)

136. *Luna d'estate* (Tosti)
V: 87242, 519 (r:170); HMV: 7-52080, DA 120 (r:170); 33: V LM-6127-16.
B-17123-3 (2/5/16) (4/16-28); B-17123-1,2 (2/5/16)

137. *Luna fedel* (Denza) (Zonophone)
Zon: X-1551; 33: Scala 825. (1902)

138. *Luna fedel* (Denza) (G&T)
G&T: 52442; RI: HMV VA 9 (r:115); 33: Rococo 2 (false start included), V LM-6127-16 (false start deleted).
2882 (11/02)

139. MACBETH: *Ah, la paterna mano* (Verdi)
V: 88558, 6014 (r:65); HMV: 2-052112, DB 118 (r:55); RI: V 15-1038 (r:34); 33: V LCT-6701-2, V LM-6127-25.
C-17197 (2/23/16) (12/16-24,6/25)

140. MADAME BUTTERFLY: *Amore o grillo* (Puccini)
(with Scotti)
V: 89043, 8014 (r:142); HMV: 2-054014, DM 113 (r:142); Ger: 78520 (r: 142).
C-8711 (3/14/10) (7/10-28)

141. MADAME BUTTERFLY: *O quanti occhi fisi* (Puccini) (with Farrar)
V: 89017, 8011 (r:145); HMV: 054201, DM 110 (r:145); Ger: 78515, 78515 (r:145); 45: V 17-0354 (in WCT-57), V ERAT-9; 33: V LCT-1037. C-6026 (3/10/08) (5/08-28,30)

142. MADAME BUTTERFLY: *Non ve l'avevo detto?* (Puccini) (with Scotti)
V: 89047, 8014 (r:140); HMV: 2-054013, DM 113 (r:140); Ger: 78520, 78520 (r:140); 33: V LM-6127-34. C-8712 (3/14/10) (8/10-28)

143. *Mamma mia, che vo' sapè* (Nutile)
V: 88206, 6009 (r:121); HMV: 2-052005, DB 119 (r:189); Ger: 76090, 85021 (r:144).
C-8344-2 (11/6/09) (12/09-33); C-8344-1 (11/6/09)

144. *Manella mia* (Valente)
V: 88465, 6025 (r:189); HMV: 2-052091, DB 121 (r:78); Ger: 76116, 85021 (r:143); RI: HMV VB 61 (r:232).
C-14358 (1/21/14) (8/14-28,30)

145. MANON: *On l'appelle Manon* (w. Farrar) (in Fr.)
V: 89059, 8011 (r:141); HMV: 2-034018, DM 110 (r:141); Ger: 78505, 78515 (r:141); 33: V LCT-6701-2. C-12750-2 (12/30/12) (3/13-28,30); C-12750-1 (12/30/12)

146. MANON: *Il sogno* (Massenet) (G&T)
G&T: 52345; RI: HMV VA 58 (r:94);
33: Rococo 2. 1785 (3/02)

147. MANON: *Il sogno* (Massenet) (Victor)
V: 81031, 523 (r:240); HMV: 2-52479,
DA 125 (r:240); Ger: 74516, 80005 (r:54);
RI: HMV VA 32 (r:158). B-1001-2 (2/9/04)
(4/04-19,22-24,6/25); B-1001-1 (2/1/04)

148. MANON: *Ah fuyez, douce image* (in French)
V: 88348, 6020 (r:111); HMV: 2-032005,
DB 130 (r:49); Ger: 76017, 85004 (r:81);
RI: V 15-1004 (r:123); 33: V LM-6127-34.
C-11422 (12/27/11) (4/12-28,30)

149. MANON LESCAUT: *Donna non vidi mai* (Puccini)
V: 87135, 505 (r:174); HMV: 7-52039,
DA 106 (r:114); Ger: 74539, 80013 (r:174);
RI: HMV VA 33 (r:54); 45: V ERAT-5;
33: V LCT-1138, V LCT-6701-2, V LM-6127-34.
B-12945 (2/24/13) (5/13-28,30)

150. *Maria, Mari* (Di Capua)
C-22127-1,2,3 (7/11/18)

151. MARTHA: *Solo, profugo, reietto* (w. Journet)
V: 89036, 8016 (r:80); HMV: 2-054010,
DM 115 (r:80); Ger: 78519, 78519 (r:80).
C-8546 (1/12/10) (3/10-26,4/27)

152. MARTHA: *Siam giunti, o giovinette* (Flotow)
(with Alda, Jacoby, Journet)
V: 95207, 10002 (r:153); HMV: 2-054030,
DM 100 (r:153); Ger: 78528, 78528 (r:155).
C-11437-2 (1/7/12) (6/12-26,4/27);
C-11437-1 (1/7/12)

153. MARTHA: *Che vuol dir ciò?* (Flotow)
(with Alda, Jacoby, Journet)
V: 95208, 10002 (r:152); HMV: 2-054031,
DM 100 (r:152); Ger: 78529, 78529 (r:154).
C-11438 (1/7/12) (6/12-26,4/27)

154. MARTHA: *Presto, presto* (Flotow)
(with Alda, Jacoby, Journet)
V: 95209, 10003 (r:155); HMV: 2-054032,
DM 101 (r:155); Ger: 78530, 78529 (r:153).
C-11439-1 (1/7/12) (6/12-30);
C-11439-2 (1/7/12)

155. MARTHA: *Dormi pur* (Flotow)
(with Alda, Jacoby, Journet)
V: 95210, 10003 (r:154); HMV: 2-054037,
DM 101 (r:154); Ger: 78531, 78528 (r:152);
RI: V 16-5002 (r:127) (in M 953); 33:
V LM-6127-34. C-11440 (1/7/12) (6/12-30)

156. MARTHA: *M'apparì* (ending "Ah, morro")
V: 88001; HMV: 052121, DB 159 (r:64);
Ger: 76065, 85011 (r:119); RI: V 15-1036
(r:93); 45: V 17-0364 (in WCT-62),
V ERAT-6; 33: V LCT-1039, V LM-6127-34.
C-3100-1 (2/11/06) (5/06-1917)

157. MARTHA: *M'apparì* (ending "Sì, morro")
V: 88001, 6002 (r:249); RR: V 7720 (r:180),
HMV DB 1802 (r:180), V 12-1015 (r:180) (in
DM 1329); 45: V 17-0112 (r:180). C-3100-2
(4/15/17) (1917-33); C-3100-3 (4/15/17)

158. *Mattinata* (Leoncavallo)
G&T: 52034, HMV DA 546 (r:178); Ger: 74511;
RI: HMV VA 32 (r:147), HMV VA 53 (r:94);
33: V LCT-1129. 2181 (4/04)

159. MEFISTOFELE: *Dai campi* (Boito) (false start)
G&T: 52348. 1789 (3/02)

160. MEFISTOFELE: *Dai campi* (no false start)
G&T: 52348, HMV DA 550 (r:161); RI: HMV
VA 7 (r:161); 33: Rococo 2. 2871 (11/02)

161. MEFISTOFELE: *Giunto sul passo estremo*
G&T: 52347, HMV DA 550 (r:160);
RI: HMV VA 7 (r:160). 1787 (3/02)

162. MESSE SOLENNELLE: *Crucifixus* (Rossini) (Lat.)
V: 87335; HMV: 7-52207, DJ 100 (r:245);
33: V LM-6127-16. B-24474-1 (9/16/20)
(4/22-26,4/27); B-24474-2 (9/16/20)

163. MESSE SOLENNELLE: *Domine Deus* (in Latin)
V: 88629, 6010 (r:7); HMV: 2-052195,
DB 120 (r:7); RI: V 11-0037 (r:201) (in
DM 1359); 45: V 17-0335 (r:30) (in WCT-35),
V 449-0014 (r:116) (in WCT-1121); 33: V
LCT-1034, V LCT-1121. C-24473-2 (9/16/20)
(6/21-28,30); C-24473-1 (9/16/20)

164. *Mia canzone, La* (Tosti) (with piano)
G&T: 52443, HMV DA 548 (r:172);
Mon: 5011, 91010; RI: HMV VA 31 (r:172).
2879 (11/02) (03-9/07)

165. *Mia canzone, La* (Tosti) (with orchestra)
V: 87213, 503 (r:21); HMV: 7-52068, DA 116
(r:102); RR: V 1688 (r:33), HMV DA 1380
(r:33); 45: V 17-0130 (r:173). B-15481-3
(1/7/15) (8/15-28); B-15481-1,2 (12/10/14)

166. *Mia sposa sarà la mia bandiera* (Rotoli)
V: 88555, 6018 (r:200); HMV: 2-052106,
DB 128 (r:200). C-17195-2 (2/23/16)
(7/16-28); C-17195-1 (2/23/16)

167. MILAGRO DE LA VIRGEN: *Flores purisimas*
(Chapi) (in Spanish)
V: 6458 (r:184); HMV: 2-062002, DB 639
(r:183); RI: HMV VB 56 (r:70). C-14662
(4/3/14) (11/28/24-28); B-14662 (4/3/14)

168. *Musica proibita* (Gastaldon)
V: 88586, 6021 (r:1); HMV: 2-052129,
DB 131 (r:1); RR: V 2212 (r:2) (10"),
HMV DA 1655 (r:2) (10").
C-15480-5 (4/15/17) (8/17-28,30);
C-15480-1,2 (12/10/14), C-15480-3,4 (1/7/15)

169. NERO: *Ah, mon sort* (Rubinstein) (in French)
V: 88589, 6017 (r:79); HMV: 2-032031,
DB 127 (r:79); RI: V 15-1039 (r:218).
C-19485-2 (4/15/17) (1/18-26,4/27);
C-19485-1 (4/15/17)

170. *Nina* (attributed to Pergolesi)
V: 87358, 519 (r:136); HMV: 7-52234,
DA 120 (r:136); RI: HMV VA 40 (r:21);
33: V LCT-1129. B-23143-4 (9/9/19)
(4/23-28); B-23143-1,2,3 (9/9/19)

171. *Noche feliz* (Posadas) (in Spanish)
V: 958 (r:258); HMV: DA 574 (r:258); RI:
V 17-5001 (r:8), V 26571 (r:8), HMV AGSA 2
(r:223); 33: V LM-6127-25. B-24460-4
(9/14/20) (12/7/23-29); B-24460-1,2,3
(9/14/20), B-24460-5,6 (9/15/20)

172. *Non t'amo più* (Denza)
G&T: 52441, DA 548 (r:164);
Mon: 5014, 91013; RI: HMV VA 31 (r:164);
33: Rococo 2. 2877 (11/02) (03-9/07)

173. *O sole mio* (Di Capua)
V: 87243, 501 (r:264); HMV: 7-52092,
DA 103 (r:264); RR: V 1616 (r:208),
HMV DA 1303 (r:208); 45: V 17-0030 (r:223)
(in WCT-7), V 17-0130 (r:165);
33: V LCT-2, HMV QKLP-501, HMV FKLP-7001,
V LM-6127-16. B-17124 (2/5/16) (5/16-40)

174. OTELLO: *Ora e per sempre addio* (Verdi)
V: 87071, 505 (r:149); HMV: 7-52017,
DA 561 (r:208); Ger: 74529, 80013 (r:149);
45: V ERAT-1. B-9743-2 (12/28/10)
(2/11-28,30) (S/8); B-9743-1 (12/28/10)

175. OTELLO: *Sì, pel ciel* (Verdi) (with Amato)
C-11285 (11/26/11)

176. OTELLO: *Sì, pel ciel* (Verdi) (with Ruffo)
V: 89075, 8045 (r: Ruffo- Credo);
HMV: 2-054049, DK 114 (r: Ruffo- Credo);
Ger: 78534, 78533 (r:63); 45: V 17-0025
(in WCT-6); 33: V LCT-1004, HMV QJLP-101,
V LM-6127-25. C-14272-1 (1/8/14)
(3/14-51); C-14272-2 (1/8/14)

177. *Over there* (Cohan) (in English and French)
V: 87294, 515 (r:102); HMV: 5-2593, DA 121
(r:21); RI: V Christmas gift 1943 (r:
Murray- Greeting), HMV VA 39 (r:182); 33:
V LM-6127-16. B-22125-4 (7/11/18) (9/18-28);
B-22125-1 (7/10/18), B-22125-2,3 (7/11/18)

178. PAGLIACCI: *Vesti la giubba* (G&T)
G&T: 52440, HMV DA 546 (r:158);
Mon: 5016, 91014; RI: HMV VA 30 (r:51);
33: Rococo 2. 2875 (11/02) (03 only)

179. PAGLIACCI: *Vesti la giubba* (with piano)
V: 81032, 930 (r:75); HMV: 52066;
45: V Christmas gift 1953 (r:203).
B-1002 (2/1/04) (4/04-11/10)

180. PAGLIACCI: *Vesti la giubba* (with orchestra)
V: 88061, 6001 (r:181); HMV: 052159,
DB 111 (r:181); Ger: 76074, 85017 (r:181);
RR: V 7720 (r:157), HMV DB 1802 (r:157),
V 12-1015 (r:157) (in DM 1329), HMV DB 2454
(fragment only); 45: V 17-0050 (r:111)
(in WCT-11), V 17-0112 (r:157), V 17-0367
(in WDM-1626), V ERAT-6; 33: V LCT-1007,
V LM-1202, HMV FJLP-5009, V LM-6127-34.
C-4317-1 (3/17/07) (7/07-3/53);
C-4317-2 (3/24/07)

181. PAGLIACCI: *No, Pagliaccio non son* (Leoncavallo)
V: 88279, 6001 (r:180); HMV: 2-052034,
DB 111 (r:180); Ger: 76095, 85017 (r:180);
45: V ERAT-1; 33: V LCT-6701-1. C-9742-2
(12/28/10) (2/11-3/53); C-9742-1 (12/28/10)

182. *Parted* (Tosti) (in English)
V: 87186, 510 (r:129); HMV: 4-2479,
DA 118 (r:193); RI: HMV VA 39 (r:177);
RR: HMV DB 3327 (r:1) (12").
B-14550 (3/9/14) (3/15-24,6/25)

183. *Partida, La* (Alvarez) (in Spanish) (w. piano)
HMV: 2-062003, DB 639 (r:167);
RI: HMV VB 55 (r:64).
C-14661-2 (4/3/14); C-14661-1 (4/3/14)

184. *Partida, La* (Alvarez) (in Spanish) (w. orch.)
V: 6458 (r:167); RI: HMV VB 58 (r:20);
33: V LM-6127-25. C-22122-1 (7/10/18)
(11/28/24-28); C-22122-2,3 (7/10/18)

185. PEARL FISHERS: *Del tempio al limitar*
(Bizet) (with Ancona)
V: 89007, 8036 (r:63); HMV: 054134, DK 116
(r:81); Ger: 78513, 78513 (r: Amato-
Brindisi). C-4327 (3/24/07) (6/07-28)

186. PEARL FISHERS: *Je crois entendre encore*
(Bizet) (in Italian)
G&T: 052066; Ger: 76062, 85006 (r:49);
RI: IRCC 61 (r:38), HMV VB 44 (r:76).
268 (1903);
C-5010 (1/10/08), C-5010-1,2 (3/16/08)

187. PEARL FISHERS: *Je crois entendre encore*
(Bizet) (in French)
V: 88580, 6026 (r:218); HMV: 2-032026,
DB 136 (r:218); RR: V 7770 (r:15),
HMV DB 1875 (r:15); 45: V 17-0052 (r:36)
(in WCT-11), V ERAT-7; 33: V LCT-1007,
HMV FJLP-5009. C-18822-3 (12/7/16)
(2/17-28,30-33); C-18822-1,2 (12/7/16)

188. PEARL FISHERS: *De mon amie, fleur endormie*
(Bizet) (in French)
V: 87269, 513 (r:225); HMV: 7-32014,
DA 114 (r:225); RI: HMV VA 36 (r:197).
B-18823-2 (12/7/16) (9/17-26,4/27);
B-18823-1 (12/7/16)

189. *Pe'chè?* (Pennino)
V: 88517, 6025 (r:144); HMV: 2-052098,
DB 119 (r:143). C-15568 (1/7/15) (3/15-28,30)

190. *Pietà, Signore* (Stradella)
V: 88599, 6024 (r:43); HMV: 2-052154,
DB 134 (r:43); RI: V 11-0036 (r:229)
(in DM 1359); 45: V 449-0013
(in WCT-1121); 33: V LCT-1121. C-22121-6
(9/26/18) (3/19-28,30); C-22121-1,2,3,4
(7/10/18), C-22121-5,7 (9/26/18)

191. *Pimpinella* (Tchaikovsky)
V: 87128, 518 (r:263); HMV: 7-52038,
DA 119 (r:263); Ger: 74538, 80016 (r:44);
RI: HMV VA 44 (r:114). B-12805-2 (1/17/13)
(4/13-11/16,22-28,30); B-12805-1 (1/17/13)

192. *Pourquoi?* (Tchaikovsky) (in French)
V: 87271, 517 (r:193); HMV: 7-32012,
DA 111 (r:129); RI: HMV VA 35 (r:193);
33: V LCT-1129. B-18656-3 (11/3/16)
(5/17-26,4/27); B-18656-1,2 (11/3/16)

193. *Pour un baiser* (Tosti) (in French)
V: 87042, 517 (r:192); HMV: 7-32000,
DA 118 (r:182); Ger: 74502, 80002 (r:33);
RI: HMV VA 35 (r:192); 45: V ERAT-1.
B-8343 (11/6/09) (12/09-26,4/27)

194. *Povero Pulcinella* (Buzzi-Peccia)
B-22518-1,2,3 (1/6/19)

195. *Première caresse* (De Crescenzo) (in French)
V: 1437 (r:22); HMV: DA 1097 (r:22);
RI: HMV AGSA 27 (r:22). B-23144-4 (9/9/19)
(1/30-11/18/32); B-23144-1,2,3 (9/9/19)

196. *Procession, La* (Franck) (in French)
V: 88556, 6035 (r:198); HMV: 2-032024,
DB 145 (r:198); RR: V 14744 (r:199),
HMV DB 3078 (r:198). C-17121-3 (2/5/16)
(9/16-26,4/27); C-17121-1,2 (2/5/16)

197. QUEEN OF SHEBA: *Magiche note* (Goldmark)
V: 87041, 520 (r:226); HMV: 7-52003,
DA 122 (r:226); Ger: 74527, 80011 (r:53);
RI: HMV VA 36 (r:188); 45: V ERAT-1.
B-6062 (11/7/09) (12/09-26,4/27);
C-6062 (3/29/08)

198. QUEEN OF SHEBA: *Inspirez-moi, race divine*
(Gounod) (in French)
V: 88552, 6035 (r:196); HMV: 2-032021,
DB 145 (r:196); RR: V 15732 (r:55),
HMV DB 3078 (r:196). C-17125-2 (2/5/16)
(4/16-26,4/27); C-17125-1 (2/5/16)

199. *Rameaux, Les* (Faure) (in French)
V: 88459, 6022 (r:116); HMV: 2-032012,
DB 132 (r:116); Ger: 76156, 85008 (r:116);
RR: V 14744 (r:196), HMV DB 3122 (r:116).
C-14201-3 (3/9/14) (6/14-28);
C-14201-1,2 (12/15/13)

200. *Régiment de Sambre et Meuse, Le*
(Planquette) (in French)
V: 88600, 6018 (r:166); HMV: 2-032042,
DB 128 (r:166). C-22516-3 (1/6/19)
(4/19-28); C-22516-1,2 (1/6/19)

201. REQUIEM: *Ingemisco* (Verdi) (in Latin)
V: 88514, 6028 (r:229); HMV: 02585,
DB 138 (r:229); RI: V 11-0037 (r:163)
(in DM 1359). C-15570-3 (1/7/15)
(4/15-28,33); C-15570-1,2 (1/7/15)

202. RIGOLETTO: *Questa o quella* (G&T)
G&T: 52344; 33: Rococo 2. 1783 (3/02)

203. RIGOLETTO: *Questa o quella* (with piano)
V: 81025, 522 (r:207); HMV: 2-52480;
45: V Christmas gift 1953 (r:179).
B-994 (2/1/04) (4/04-7/09,22-24,6/25)

204. RIGOLETTO: *Questa o quella* (with orchestra)
V: 87018, 500 (r:208); HMV: 2-52642,
DA 102 (r:30); Ger: 74523, 80009 (r:30);
45: V 17-0044 (in WCT-10),
V 17-0132 (r:208), V ERAT-4;
33: V LCT-1006, HMV FJLP-5004, V LM-6127-16.
B-6035 (3/16/08) (6/08-40)

205. RIGOLETTO: *Parmi veder le lagrime* (Verdi)
V: 88429, 6016 (r:77); HMV: 2-052076,
DB 126 (r:77); Ger: 76111, 85019 (r:249);
RR: V 11-8112 (r:77), HMV DB 3903 (r:77);
45: V 17-0131 (r:77). C-11421-2 (2/24/13)
(6/13-3/52); C-11421-1 (12/27/11)

206. RIGOLETTO: *La donna è mobile* (Zonophone)
Zon: X-1555; 33: Scala 825. (1902)

207. RIGOLETTO: *La donna è mobile* (with piano)
V: 81026, 522 (r:203); HMV: 52062.
B-995 (2/1/04) (4/04-7/09,22-24,6/25)

208. RIGOLETTO: *La donna è mobile* (with orch.)
V: 87017, 500 (r:204); HMV: 2-52641,
DA 561 (r:174); Ger: 74522, 80007 (r:250);
RR: V 1616 (r:173), HMV DA 1303 (r:173);
45: V 17-0049 (r:77) (in WCT-11), V 49-1420
(in WDM-1438), V 17-0132 (r:204), V ERAT-4;
33: V LCT-1007, HMV FJLP-5009, V LM-6127-16.
B-6033 (3/16/08) (6/08-40)

209. RIGOLETTO: *Quartet* (Verdi)
(with Abott, Homer, Scotti)
V: 96000, 10011 (r:88); HMV: 054117, DO 100
(r:88); Ger: 79000, 79000 (r: Chaliapin-
Don Carlos); RI: HMV DB 2454 (fragment
only). C-4259 (2/20/07) (3/07-24,6/25)

210. RIGOLETTO: *Quartet* (Verdi)
(with Sembrich, Jacoby, Scotti)
C-5053-1,2 (2/3/08)

211. RIGOLETTO: *Quartet* (Verdi)
(with Sembrich, Severina, Scotti)
V: 96001, 10001 (r:131); HMV: 054199,
DQ 101 (r:131); Ger: 79001, 79001 (r:39);
RI: V 16-5001 (r:39) (in M 953). C-5053-3
(2/7/08) (4/08-24,6/25); C-5053-4 (2/7/08)

212. RIGOLETTO: *Quartet* (Verdi)
(with Tetrazzini, Jacoby, Amato)
HMV: 2-054038; Ger: 79003 (r:131);
RI: IRCC 36 (r: Destinn- Ebben),
V 15-1019 (r: Melba- Alerte).
C-11447-4 (2/13/12); C-11447-1 (1/10/12),
C-11447-2 (1/19/12), C-11447-3 (2/13/12)

213. RIGOLETTO: *Quartet* (Verdi)
(with Galli-Curci, Perini, De Luca)
V: 95100, 10000 (r:133); HMV: 2-054066,
DQ 100 (r:133); 45: V 17-0017 (r:217)
(in WCT-4), V ERAT-8; 33: V LCT-1003,
V LM-6127-16. C-19132-2 (1/25/17)
(4/17-9/52); C-19132-1,3 (1/25/17)

214. *Rosary, The* (Nevin) (in English)
B-17196-1,2,3,4 (2/23/16),
B-17196-5,6 (3/20/16)

215. *Rose, a kiss, and you, A* (Souci) (in Eng.)
B-22517-1,2 (1/6/19), B-22517-3,4 (2/10/19)

216. SALVATOR ROSA: *Mia piccirella* (Gomez)
V: 88638, 6034 (r:78); HMV: 2-052224,
DB 144 (r:14). C-23150 (9/11/19)
(10/22-28); B-23150 (9/11/19)

217. SAMSON AND DELILAH: *Je viens célébrer la victoire* (with Homer, Journet) (in French)
V: 89088, 10010 (r:127); HMV: 2-034026, DM 126 (r:127); RI: V 16-5003 (r:92) (in M 953); 45: V 17-0017 (r:213) (in WCT-4); 33: V LCT-1003. C-22575-2 (2/10/19) (5/19-26,4/27); C-22575-1,3 (2/10/19)

218. SAMSON AND DELILAH: *Vois ma misère, hélas* (Saint-Saëns) (in French)
V: 88581, 6026 (r:187); HMV: 2-032029, DB 136 (r:187); RI: V 15-1039 (r:169). C-18821-1 (12/7/16) (4/17-28,30-33); C-18821-2 (12/7/16)

219. *Sancta Maria* (Faure) (in French)
V: 88559, 6029 (r:45); HMV: 2-032037, DB 139 (r:45). C-17342-2 (3/20/16) (1/17-28); C-17342-1 (3/20/16)

220. *Santa Lucia* (anonymous)
V: 88560, 6032 (r:59); HMV: 2-052107, DB 142 (r:59); RR: HMV DB 2991 (r:5). C-17344 (3/20/16) (10/16-33)

221. SCHIAVO: *Quando nascesti tu* (Gomez)
V: 88345, 6027 (r:32); HMV: 2-052062, DB 137 (r:32); Ger: 76105, 85031 (r:32). C-11273-2 (11/19/11) (9/12-11/14,22-28); C-11273-1 (11/19/11)

222. *Scordame* (Fucito)
V: 1007 (r:224); HMV: DA 608 (r:224); RI: HMV VA 43 (r:224). B-23152 (9/11/19) (6/6/24-28)

223. *Sei morta nella vita mia* (Costa)
V: 87293; RI: V Christmas gift 1947, HMV AGSA 2 (r:171); 45: V 17-0030 (r:173) (in WCT-7); 33: V LCT-1, HMV QKLP-501, HMV FKLP-7001, V LM-6127-16. B-21774-2 (4/16/18); B-21774-1 (4/16/18)

224. *Senza nisciuno* (De Curtis)
V: 1007 (r:222); HMV: DA 608 (r:222); RI: HMV VA 43 (r:222). B-23149-4 (9/11/19) (6/6/24-28); B-23149-1,2,3 (9/11/19)

225. *Sérénade de Don Juan* (Tchaikovsky) (in Fr.)
V: 87175, 513 (r:188); HMV: 7-32006, DA 114 (r:188); Ger: 74504, 80004 (r:266); RI: HMV VA 42 (r:226); 33: V LCT-1129. B-14355 (1/21/14) (5/14-26,4/27)

226. *Sérénade espagnole* (Ronald) (in French)
V: 87169, 520 (r:197); HMV: 7-32008, DA 122 (r:197); RI: HMV VA 42 (r:225). B-14359-3 (3/9/14) (10/14-11/16,22-26,4/27); B-14359-1 (1/21/14), B-14359-2 (3/9/14)

227. *Serenata* (Memories of a concert) (Bracco)
V: 88628, 6033 (r:232); HMV: 2-052191, DB 143 (r:232); RI: HMV VB 62 (r:121); 33: V LCT-1129. C-23151-1 (9/11/19) (4/21/28); B-23151 (9/11/19), C-23151-2 (9/11/19)

228. *Si vous l'aviez compris* (Denza) (accompanied by Elman) (in French)
V: 89084, 8008 (r:62); HMV: 2-032018, DK 104 (r:62). C-15682-3 (2/6/15) (6/15-30); C-15682-1,2 (2/6/15)

229. STABAT MATER: *Cujus animam* (Rossini) (in Lat.)
V: 88460, 6028 (r:201); HMV: 2-052086, DB 138 (r:201); Ger: 76114, 85027 (r:1); RI: V 11-0036 (r:190) (in DM 1359). C-14200-1 (12/15/13) (9/14-28,33); C-14200-2 (12/15/13)

230. *Sultanto a te* (Fucito)
V: 1117 (r:262); HMV: DA 754 (r:262); RR: HMV DA 1367 (r:262). B-22515-5 (2/10/19) (11/27/25-28); B-22515-1,2,3,4 (1/6/19)

231. *Tarantella sincera* (De Crescenzo)
V: 88347, 6031 (r:61); HMV: 2-052067, DB 141 (r:61); Ger: 76109, 85035 (r:61). C-11472 (1/19/12) (4/12-28,5/19/33-5/34)

232. *Tiempo antico* (Caruso)
V: 88472, 6033 (r:227); HMV: 2-052108, DB 143 (r:227); RI: HMV VB 61 (r:144); 33: V LCT-1129. C-17343-2 (3/20/16) (6/16-28); C-17343-1 (3/20/16)

233. TOSCA: *Recondita armonia* (with piano)
V: 81029; HMV: 52191; RI: HMV VA 34 (r:240). B-999 (2/1/04) (4/04-7/09)

234. TOSCA: *Recondita armonia* (with orchestra)
V: 87043, 511 (r:241); HMV: 7-52004, DA 112 (r:241); Ger: 74528, 80010 (r:241); RR: V 11-8569 (r: Bori- Sempre) (12"), HMV DB 2644 (r:7) (12"); 45: V 17-0020 (in WCT-5), V ERAT-5, V ERA-181; 33: V LCT-1, V LM-6127-34. B-8347 (11/6/09) (12/09-40)

235. TOSCA: *Perchè chiuso?* (with Farrar)
C-11618-1,2 (2/27/12)

236. TOSCA: *Or lasciami al lavoro* (with Farrar)
C-11619 (2/27/12)

237. TOSCA: *E lucevan le stelle* (AICC)
AICC: 84004 (cylinder); Pathé: 84004 (single or r: 117 or 260 or Schwarz- Jerum) (vertically cut); Emerson: 301 (incomplete) (vertically cut); Herrold: 500 (r: Clement- Green); RI: IRCC 3121 (r: Cotogni- Mulattieri); 33: Royale 1632, Scala 825. (c.1901)

238. TOSCA: *E lucevan le stelle* (Zonophone)
Zon: X-1553; 33: Rococo 2, Scala 825. (1902)

239. TOSCA: *E lucevan le stelle* (G&T)
G&T: 52349, HMV DA 547 (r:109); Mon: 5010, 91009; RI: HMV VA 29 (r:109). 1790 (3/02) (03 only)

240. TOSCA: *E lucevan le stelle* (with piano)
V: 81028, 523 (r:147); HMV: 52063, DA 125 (r:147); RI: HMV VA 34 (r:233). B-998 (2/1/04) (4/04-7/09,22-24,6/25)

241. TOSCA: *E lucevan le stelle* (with orchestra)
V: 87044, 511 (r:234); HMV: 7-52002, DA 112 (r:234); Ger: 74526, 80010 (r:234); 45: V 17-0336 (r:8) (in WCT-35), V ERAT-5; 33: V LCT-1034. B-8346 (11/6/09) (12/09-40) (S/8)

242. TOSCA: *Ah, franchigia a Floria Tosca*
(Puccini) (with Farrar)
C-11620 (2/27/12)

243. TOSCA: *O dolci mani* (Puccini) (with Farrar)
C-11621 (2/27/12)

244. TOSCA: *Amaro sol per te m'era il morire*
(Puccini) (with Farrar)
C-11622 (2/27/12)

245. TRAVIATA: *Brindisi* (Verdi) (with Gluck)
V: 87511, 3031 (r:250); HMV: 7-54006,
DJ 100 (r:162); 45: V 17-0353 (in WCT-57),
V ERAT-9; 33: V LCT-1037, V LM-6127-16.
B-14729-2 (4/20/14) (12/14-30);
B-14729-1,3 (4/20/14)

246. *Triste ritorno* (Barthélemy)
V: 88048, 6030 (r:261); HMV: 052153,
DB 140 (r:95); Ger: 76070, 85005 (r:3).
C-4159 (12/30/06) (3/07-11/15,22-26,4/27)

247. TROVATORE: *Mal reggendo* (Verdi) (w. Homer)
V: 89049, 8013 (r:255); HMV: 2-054017,
DM 112 (r:255); Ger: 78524, 78514 (r:255).
C-6682-2 (12/29/10) (3/11-28);
C-6682-1 (12/19/08)

248. TROVATORE: *Perigliarti ancor languente*
(Verdi) (with Homer)
C-6680 (12/19/08)

249. TROVATORE: *Ah sì, ben mio, coll'essere*
V: 88121, 6002 (r:157); HMV: 052210,
DB 112 (r:97); Ger: 76079, 85019 (r:205);
45: V 17-0338 (r:264) (in WCT-35), V ERAT-4;
33: V LCT-1034. C-6034 (3/16/08) (6/08-33)

250. TROVATORE: *Di quella pira* (Verdi)
V: 87001, 512 (r:30), 3031 (r:245);
HMV: 2-52489, DA 113 (r:124); Ger: 74518,
80007 (r:208); 45: V 17-0128 (r:49),
V 17-0339 (r:57) (in WCT-35), V ERAT-4;
33: V LCT-1034, V LM-6127-16.
B-3103 (2/11/06) (5/06-30) (S/8)

251. TROVATORE: *Miserere* (with Gadski)
C-8352-1,2 (11/7/09)

252. TROVATORE: *Miserere* (w. Alda) (without chorus)
C-8506-1 (12/27/09)

253. TROVATORE: *Miserere* (w. Alda) (with chorus)
V: 89030, 8042 (r:256); HMV: 2-054007,
DK 119 (r:256); Ger: 78518, 78518 (r:256);
45: V 17-0018 (r:31) (in WCT-4);
33: V LCT-1003. C-8506-3 (1/6/10)
(2/10-3/53) (S/8); C-8506-2 (1/6/10)

254. TROVATORE: *Ai nostri monti* (Verdi) (with
Homer) (Caruso goes down on last note.)
V: 89018; HMV: 054198; 33: V LM-6127-16.
C-6036-1 (3/17/08) (6/08-1911)

255. TROVATORE: *Ai nostri monti* (Verdi) (with
Homer) (Caruso goes up on last note.)
V: 89018, 8013 (r:247); HMV: 054198,
DM 112 (r:247); Ger: 78514, 78514 (r:247).
C-6036-2 (12/29/10) (1911-28)

256. TROVATORE: *Ai nostri monti* (Verdi) (with
Schumann-Heink)
V: 89060, 8042 (r:253); HMV: 2-054042,
DK 119 (r:253); Ger: 78532, 78518 (r:253);
45: V ERAT-9; 33: V LCT-1138. C-12804-2
(1/17/13) (4/13-3/53); C-12804-1 (1/17/13)

257. *Trusting eyes* (Gartner) (in English)
V: 87187, 514 (r:266); HMV: 4-2480,
DA 115 (r:266); RR: HMV DA 1656 (r:266).
B-14203-4 (3/9/14) (3/15-26,4/27);
B-14203-1 (12/15/13), C-14203 (1/21/14),
B-14203-3 (1/21/14)

258. *Tu, ca nun chiagne* (De Curtis)
V: 958 (r:171); HMV: DA 574 (r:171);
RI: HMV VA 41 (r:263).
B-23141 (9/8/19) (12/7/23-29)

259. *Tu- Habanera* (Fuentes) (in Spanish)
B-14663-1,2 (4/3/14)

260. *Tu non mi vuoi più bene* (Pini-Corsi)
AICC: 84003 (cylinder); Pathé: 84003
(single or r: 117 or 237) (vertically cut);
CRS: 6 (r:117); 33: Rare Records M302,
Scala 825. (c.1901)

261. *Uocchie celeste* (De Crescenzo)
V: 88587, 6030 (r:246); HMV: 2-052149,
DB 115 (r:119); RI: HMV VB 59 (r:56);
33: V LCT-1129. C-19483-2 (4/15/17)
(4/18-26,4/27); C-19483-1 (4/15/17)

262. *Vaghissima sembianza* (Donaudy)
V: 1117 (r:230); HMV: DA 754 (r:230);
RR: HMV DA 1367 (r:230); 45: V 17-0337
(r:35) (in WCT-35); 33: V LCT-1034,
V LM-6127-25. B-24463-4 (9/15/20)
(11/27/25-28); B-24463-1,2,3 (9/15/20)

263. *Vieni sul mar* (anonymous)
V: 87305, 518 (r:191); HMV: DA 119 (r:191);
RI: HMV VA 41 (r:258); 33: V LCT-1129,
V LM-6127-16. B-23139-2 (9/8/19)
(2/20-28,30); B-23139-1 (9/8/19)

264. *Vucchella, 'A* (Tosti)
V: 87304, 501 (r:173); HMV: 7-52162,
DA 103 (r:173); 45: V 17-0338 (r:249)
(in WCT-35); 33: V LCT-1034. B-23138-3
(9/8/19) (12/19-40); B-23138-1,2,4 (9/8/19)

265. XERXES: *Ombra mai fu* (Handel)
V: 88617, 6023 (r:128); HMV: 2-052180,
DB 133 (r:128); RR: V 8806 (r:128),
HMV DB 2073 (r:128); 45: V 17-0033 (r:27)
(in WCT-7), V ERAT-6; 33: V LCT-2,
HMV QKLP-501, HMV FKLP-7001,
V LM-6127-25. C-23714-5 (1/29/20)
(7/20-28,30-33); C-23714-1,2,3,4 (1/29/20)

266. *Your eyes have told me what I did not know*
(O'Hara) (in English)
V: 87159, 514 (r:257); HMV: 4-2375,
DA 115 (r:257); Ger: 74599, 80004 (r:225);
RR: HMV DA 1656 (r:257); 45: V Christmas
gift 1951 (r:1). B-13106-2 (4/10/13)
(7/13-26,4/27); B-13106-1 (4/10/13)